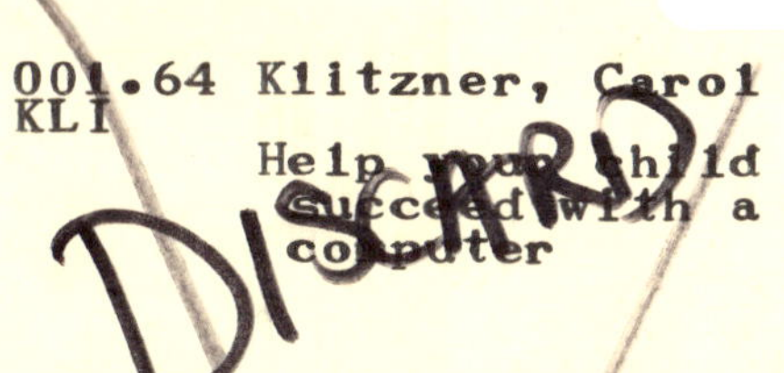

001.64 Klitzner, Carol
KLI

Help your child
succeed with a
computer

DISCARD

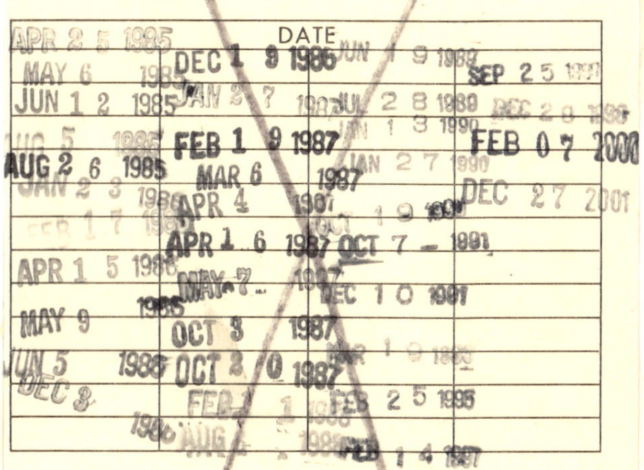

	DATE		
APR 2 5 1985	DEC 1 9 1986	JUN 1 9 1989	SEP 2 5 1991
MAY 6 1985	JAN 2 7 1987	JUL 2 8 1989	DEC 2 0 1996
JUN 1 2 1985	FEB 1 9 1987	JUN 1 3 1990	FEB 0 7 2000
AUG 5 1985	MAR 6 1987	JAN 2 7 1990	DEC 2 7 2001
AUG 2 6 1985	APR 4 1987	OCT 1 9 1990	
JAN 2 3 1986	APR 1 6 1987	OCT 7 1991	
FEB 1 7 1986	MAY 7 1987	DEC 1 0 1991	
APR 1 5 1986	OCT 3 1987		
MAY 9 1986	OCT 3 0 1987	APR 1 9 1989	
JUN 5 1986	FEB 1 1988	FEB 2 5 1995	
DEC 3 1986	AUG 4 1988	FEB 1 4 1997	

HOOD COUNTY LIBRARY

© THE BAKER & TAYLOR CO.

CHOOSING AND USING THE
RIGHT COMPUTER FOR YOUR CHILD

Help Your Child Succeed with a Computer

Carol and Herbert Klitzner

Simon and Schuster *New York*

Copyright © 1984 by Carol Klitzner and Herbert Klitzner
All rights reserved
including the right of reproduction
in whole or in part in any form
Published by Simon and Schuster
A Division of Simon & Schuster, Inc.
Simon & Schuster Building
Rockefeller Center
1230 Avenue of the Americas
New York, New York 10020
SIMON AND SCHUSTER and colophon are registered trademarks of
Simon & Schuster, Inc.
Designed by Irving Perkins
Manufactured in the United States of America
10 9 8 7 6 5 4 3 2 1

Library of Congress Cataloging in Publication Data

Klitzner, Carol, 1946–
    Help your child succeed with a computer.
    Includes index.
    1. Computers and children.   2. Microcomputers.
I. Klitzner, Herb.   II. Title.
QA76.9.C659K55   1984   001.64   84-13847
ISBN: 0-671-49418-X

Acknowledgments

We want to express our thanks to all the parents, grandparents, and children, both those with computers and those thinking about buying them, who took the time to speak to us when we were writing this book. Their insights and concerns were invaluable to us in finding out what is on parents' minds when they think about their children, computers, and the future. We would also like to thank the teachers and researchers from a variety of different backgrounds whom we spoke with for sharing their experiences and ideas with us.

We also thank Jan Burdick, who helped with the research and found so much valuable information for us, and our editor, Bob Bender, for his understanding and help as we worked on the book.

To our parents

Carl and Margaret
and
Joseph and Irene

Contents

The Kid–Computer Connection

BUYING A COMPUTER FOR A CHILD IS UNIQUE

Buying a computer for your child is not like buying a pair of jeans. You can't walk into a computer store and look for a size 4-Tall or 14-Slim. Ideally, a computer will "fit" your child, but the fit is more complex than a fit tailored to height or age. The best computer for your child will fit his or her interests, likes and dislikes, personality, strengths, and weaknesses, as well as the whole family's needs—and your pocketbook. Can you select among different computers guided by the differences among children? We believe the answer is yes, and we believe that this point of view helps you to move the focus from technology back onto the child, where it belongs. When you select a computer by picking a good "fit" for your child, your child will get the most out of owning that computer.

One reason that buying a computer is unique is that a computer is a rather unique object in your child's world. A computer is not a toy, but it's fun. It's not a textbook, but it can teach your child. It's something your child can use, and yet the same computer can be used by adults as well. Your child can play games on the computer or he can program his own games. A computer is one of the most flexible tools a child can have.

When your child uses a computer, he will be gaining familiarity with computer technology and probably gaining skill in other areas as well. He'll also be putting something of himself into what he does, perhaps by creating computer programs or computer graphics or by finding ways to use the computer to help with homework or hobbies. The patterns of tasks he uses it for will be an individual one. In a sense, a computer *is* whatever your child defines that computer to be. As a parent, you help make that definition.

SUCCEEDING WITH A COMPUTER

What Parents Want

What prompted you to begin thinking about buying a computer for your child? If you're like many parents, the first impetus was your feeling that from the office to school to home, computers are fast becoming a fact of modern life, and your wish that your child be comfortable with this modern tool. Many parents feel that their child's knowledge of computer skills will help insure success in a career.

Parents also feel that using the computer as an educational tool can help their child succeed in school. In fact, for many parents, the most powerful impetus for seriously considering getting a home computer is seeing their child using a computer at school.

Certainly it's true that a computer can help your child understand technology and attain the goals of academic and job success, but it's too easy to think of success with computers in this rather narrow way. As a parent, you have a variety of goals for your child, and you should look upon a computer as possibly helping your child to reach a number of these goals. We feel that computers can help your child move closer to goals like the ones on the following list.

Goals for academic development:

- Skills in specific subject areas.
- Computer literacy skills.
- Problem-solving ability.

Goals for personal expression:

• Creativity, skill, and insight in music, art, or writing.

Goals for personality development:

• Self-discipline, persistence, orderliness, and organizational skill.
• Self-reliance and independence.
• Self-esteem and confidence.

Social goals:

• Cooperation and the ability to work together with others. (You may be surprised to see that computers can help foster cooperative behavior, but they can, as you'll discover below.)

Career goals:

• Career skills and financial independence.

A computer alone doesn't automatically create these results, but it provides an environment and an opportunity that your child can take advantage of. As you read this book, each of these areas will be dealt with, and you'll see how this can be true.

Some Children's Experiences

Let's look at how some young people have found computers helpful. You'll see that in each of these examples the child has moved closer to some important goal.

Jennifer is a four-year-old who plays a preschool game her parents bought her to use on her older brother's computer. She sees a letter at the top of the screen and picks its match from a group of letters at the bottom. She's learning to recognize the shapes of different letters of the alphabet. Being familiar with the shapes and being able to tell them apart will help her when she learns to read in school. Jennifer can also play games for young children that help her to count groups of pictures on the screen, games that help her match colors, or games that teach her about different geometric shapes.

Steve is a college senior at an Eastern university. Last year he and two partners started a programming business with their microcomputers. Not only did the business make a profit that helped pay for college and future business school expenses, but it helped Steve decide on a career involving the business uses of computers—a clear case of a computer helping pave the way to financial independence and career success.

Susan is a ten-year-old who uses a music synthesizer attached to her family's computer. The synthesizer has a piano-like keyboard that Susan can play as she composes songs. She composes her own songs, stores them on the computer disk, and hears them played back by the synthesizer. Susan can tell the synthesizer what instruments to imitate so that she can hear her song played by instruments with different qualities. Susan's musical knowledge and her ear for music have improved along with her compositions.

Sean, who's fourteen, has always had trouble with written assignments. His handwriting is poor, and because he also doesn't take the time to make his thoughts clear, he tends to scribble the first thing that comes into his head and turn that in as a final draft. Recently, Sean began using a word processor on a home computer. He has found the computer itself and the editing techniques in the word processor interesting enough that he now regularly rereads and edits his papers to make them clearer and better. The final product from the computer's printer is neat enough to satisfy any teacher.

James is a teenage boy with a profound hearing loss. Because of his poor performance in school so far, his teachers have not expected him to achieve much academically. When James began to learn computer programming along with another hearing-impaired student, his progress in programming surprised his teachers. James apparently had intellectual capabilities that went unused and unrecognized until he was presented with a tool and a task that intrigued him. Another benefit of the computer is that it has given James and the other hearing-impaired student a reason to communicate intensively as they work to solve problems with their computer programs. Developing communication skills in hearing-impaired students is an important concern of teachers and parents.

Eleven-year-old Eric uses his computer to play games. But the games he plays are ones that he finds listed in computer magazines and types into the computer himself. Some of the programs he types are very long, but Eric has found the motivation and persistence to work at each project until he's finished. He has gained organizational skills and learned to set goals for himself each day. In addition, he has had to use problem-solving skills to determine what to do to modify those commands in the programs that don't work on his type of computer.

These children have "succeeded" in different ways. They have each gained something from using a computer. While a computer is not a cure-all or a substitute for other experiences in these children's lives, it has had positive effects.

OUR VIEWS ON HOW COMPUTERS HELP CHILDREN

We think that computers can help in a variety of areas and that some of the most important benefits your child can gain from a computer are things most parents don't think of at first.

When computers are used creatively in education they can make real intellectual growth possible. For example, science teachers report that some uses of computers in science, such as those in which students interact with a model of a scientific law in operation, really help students develop insight into complex scientific processes and abstract concepts.

Many teachers report that they see a tremendous increase in motivation when computers are on the scene. Students who used to be uninterested in school begin showing up early in the morning or staying late so they can work on computer projects.

Working, playing, and wrestling with a computer produces a blend of feelings of challenge and control that a child rarely finds in so concentrated a form elsewhere in his experience. Children respond well to this, and the benefits to their self-image of controlling a powerful tool, overcoming problems, and meeting with success can be great.

We feel that computers can foster cooperative behavior. While many people worry that working at a computer can turn a child into a person who communicates better with machines than with human beings, research done by the Bank Street College of Education suggests that computers, instead, offer children an opportunity for interaction and collaboration. In the classrooms the researchers studied, there was more discussion of tasks and more collaboration among children when they were working on computer tasks than at other times. This confirms the observations of many teachers that computers become a hobby that draws many students together to share a common interest and to help each other solve problems. Similar patterns of talking and working together have been repeatedly observed even among kindergarten and preschool children who are working on simple projects.

We think that computer programming allows children to explore a new system of reasoning. Many experts say that the kind of careful planning and reasoning that goes into good computer programming will help children to develop intellectually in ways that they wouldn't without a computer, and that this will help them in other areas where problem-solving skills are needed. While studies have not yet shown a general carry-over of skills from computer activities to other intellectual tasks, we feel that it is beneficial to children to program computers just for the experience of working in a new and logical domain of knowledge.

The most exciting area of computer use to us is the creative area. While computers are valuable as teaching tools for traditional school subjects, they can be astonishingly helpful in more expressive endeavors. Word processors, music synthesizers, and computer graphics are some of the most advanced creative tools available to professional writers, musicians, and artists today, and children have access to all of these through an inexpensive home computer. Computers are having a profound impact on the way children express themselves through art, music, and writing.

Even when computers are used for a less expressive kind of writing, they can change the way young people approach writing. All the students in freshman English at one Western university have begun to use a writing analysis tool on a computer to help improve their compositions. The teacher in charge of this project has found that with this tool the improvement in his ability to teach writing and set standards for good writing is truly dramatic. He finds that for the first time he is confident of his ability to help students improve their writing. For the students, the computer has transformed a frustrating task into a rewarding one.

We are also impressed by the potential of computers to further a child's accomplishments in almost any area that interests him. As we've said, a computer is flexible, and each child will use it in his own way. When a child is encouraged to use a computer as a tool in areas that are already interesting to him, he is likely to be interested in the computer also and to benefit from using it.

Finally, we've seen that computers can give a family a new common interest. Children and their parents can share this new hobby, working to solve problems, learning from each other, and enjoying the computer together. Older children frequently act as tutors to their younger siblings or help them out with their computer activities.

SELECTING A COMPUTER

Buying a computer and helping your child use it necessarily involves you in a whole new world of computer technology, and many parents are not comfortable in this world. Perhaps you feel that it's going to be hard to help your child learn about computers because you'll have to learn so much yourself. It's true that you'll have to learn the basics of "hardware" and "software," and we will cover these basics in the book. But you won't have to become an expert in technology.

Even with a knowledge of computers, it may be hard for many parents to understand what their child will do with this new tool. We'll show you the wide variety of activities a child might engage in with a computer. And we'll help you to see which computer activities tie in well with your child's interests, career goals, academic needs, and individual style.

Once you know what your child will do with a computer, you can pick the computer that facilitates those activities. We'll show you how to do this and also help you see how to balance your child's needs against real-life constraints, such as money or the need for several children to share a computer. We'll give you guidance in picking computer equipment for children with physical disabilities as well.

In making any purchase for a child, you have to take the child's wishes and plans into consideration. In buying a computer, you need to evaluate your child's choices and reasons to see if they make good sense. We'll try to give you some useful guidance for the whole process of discussion with your child.

It can be difficult to understand what to do in a computer store to become familiar with the specific hardware and software you're interested in and to evaluate their usefulness to your child. We'll show you how to handle yourself in a computer store.

Finally, once you put a computer in your home, the real growth process can begin. You'll need to help your child decide on computer projects, help the child manage them, and help him channel his enthusiasm into constructive channels. We'll show you how, as a parent, you can guide your child's growth so that he gets the most from this new experience.

YOU'RE NOT IN THIS ALONE

It's hard to find parents these days who have not either bought or thought about buying a computer for their child. In making a decision on a computer, it may help to talk to parents or teachers who have first-hand experience with the computers you're considering, the software you want, and the stores and service centers in your area. Someone who has a computer can often tell you a good deal about what it will and won't do.

Once you've bought a computer for your child, you'll probably find that you're very concerned about the use of computers at your child's school. You'll want support in the school for the things you're trying to do at home—programming classes, educational software to take home on loan from the library or classroom, computer clubs for your child, and so on. You'll be very glad at that point to have fellow parents who can work with you. By pooling your insights and sharing your experience, knowledge, and ideas, you can help develop a plan for computer use that is right for your community.

WHERE TO START

Before you can involve your child in the world of computers, you need to get a clear picture of how your child can best use a computer. In the next chapter, you'll begin the process by seeing the range of activities children become involved in with computers and the benefits they get from these activities.

CHAPTER 2

How a Child Grows with a Computer

Children use computers for a very broad range of activities, from programming the computer itself to using it as an artistic medium. In this chapter we want to give you a feeling for what computer activities are possible and how these uses of the computer could benefit your child.

Computers can be an end in themselves, as they are to a child who is interested in programming. The boy who learns to program the computer to create his own video games will learn more about computers than he could ever learn from a book on the subject. He'll learn how tasks must be structured for a computer and how to think logically about writing a computer program. In addition, he'll have the satisfaction of mastering a new skill, one that's valued by society.

For many, if not most children, though, computers will also be a tool that helps them do other tasks and learn other skills. The girl who uses the computer to improve her math skills is using the computer as a tool. So is the boy who uses it as a music synthesizer to play his own compositions. The child who uses a computer in this manner will benefit in two ways: by becoming better at the particular skill and by becoming familiar and comfortable with computers. Often children also find that they can do things in a new way with a computer. They can explore areas that were previously not available to them or see familiar things in a brand new way, as when they use a computer to simulate a science experiment, to draw or "paint" pictures on the screen, or to create colorful animations.

In the next section, we'll introduce you to children who are using computers for a variety of activities, and show you what the computer has meant to them. Very often, the true importance of the computer activity is not what you'd think at first.

WHAT CHILDREN DO WITH COMPUTERS

Exploring Music with a Computer

Michael is a 10-year-old who takes music lessons from a piano teacher who has him play the piano for half of the lesson and use a music synthesizer attached to a home computer for the other half. Michael is an expressive child, and he's found composing music on the synthesizer a satisfying experience. He began with a song just a few notes long. Three or four months later he was writing much more complex compositions that he planned out in advance at home, including several pieces connected by a common idea. At each lesson he insists on hearing his first piece over again, because even such a very simple piece has meaning for its creator. He gets great pleasure from seeing how far he's come.

Michael can hear each of his compositions on a range of instruments imitated by the synthesizer. He can listen to piano, violin, clarinet, and so forth, and become sensitive to the different qualities of each instrument. He remembers these qualities. When he gets a new musical idea, he knows which instrument sound will best express that idea for him. His teacher, whose students range from first to sixth graders, feels that the computer and synthesizer are excellent ear-training and composing tools that give her students a broader musical education than they would get with traditional music lessons. She also reports that children have more interest in their music and a longer attention span when they use the computer synthesizer. They even practice both piano and composition at home without their parents' urging.

Getting Feedback from a Computer

Many students use a word-processor software package on a home computer for writing, and teachers report that these students typically are enthusiastic about their writing and often show real improvement. The word processor allows the child to type a story into the computer, easily make changes in the work as she enters it, and print a copy on a printer. Later, she can retrieve the story as often as needed, making further changes and printing new copies. Children are willing to make the kinds of spelling, grammar, and structural changes in their writing that teachers suggest because they won't have the drudgery of recopying the whole story. These improvements have come to be expected, but one junior-high student found that his writing benefited from the computer in a rather unusual way.

Jimmy had a running conflict with his teachers, particularly in English and social studies. They told him that his writing assignments were not at the level they expected from a bright junior-high student. When his writing didn't change, they told him he was being stubborn and not working hard enough.

Then one teacher decided to put a piece of Jimmy's writing through a computer's "readability program"—a program designed to tell a teacher the reading level of a passage from a book so the teacher can judge whether it's suitable for a class. Jimmy's work was judged by the computer to be at the second or third grade level. When his teacher showed him the result, Jimmy believed for the first time that he had a problem. After all, a computer had said so. Then he asked how the computer could tell the reading level. The teacher explained that the computer looked at such things as sentence length and the number of syllables in the words.

Jimmy went home and worked on his writing for a week on his own, for the first time consciously thinking about such things as choice of words and complexity of sentences and ideas. He showed the results to his teacher, who found that Jimmy's writing had improved. For the first time, Jimmy had been given a quantified appraisal of his work along with a set of standards by which the work could be judged. He was able to use this new information to improve his performance. Of course, not all aspects of good writing are measurable in this way, but for Jimmy it was a starting point.

Computer feedback like this has an impact on children in many other areas as well. Children who work on the computer in what are called "simulations" are working on real-life situations such as presidential elections, the problems of feeding a large population, or managing the ecology of a pond. Facts, choice points, and the results of decisions are presented by the computer. As children make decisions, they see the results on the computer screen immediately. In an election simulation, for example, children see what happens if they advertise on television, campaign in different states, take certain positions, get important endorsements, and so forth. This kind of role-playing teaches children about the electoral process as no lecture by a teacher ever will. Computer simulations can be simplistic, but they allow children to work directly with important principles and constraints, see their consequences, and build understanding of a subject area.

Success at Programming

Eight-year-old David didn't care much about schoolwork and spent much of his time teasing other children in his class instead of working. As a result, he was not popular with the other children and not successful in his studies. Computers were introduced into the class, and all the children were taught programming. To his teacher's surprise, David immediately took to the computer, quickly mastering new commands and writing programs. David volunteered to teach other children programming, and was successful at this as well. He had found an area that motivated him enough to work hard and one in which he had a natural aptitude. For a child who had not shown much interest in school or experienced success before, this was a real breakthrough.

From David's point of view, however, the best result of his new skill may be the respect he now has from other children in his class. They come to him for help with their programs, and David has found that he can help them and get along with them. He has cut down on his teasing and is instead learning to enjoy working with his classmates.

Learning a Skill Not Taught in School

Carla is a thirteen-year-old who finds copying papers over by hand laborious and difficult, because her handwriting is not good. Her parents are anxious for her to learn to type, so that she can either use their typewriter for her papers or use a computer word processor efficiently. However, her school does not teach typing. Because Carla has a home computer, her parents bought several typing-tutorial software packages for her. With the packages, she is learning to type.

One of the packages teaches typing in the traditional way by presenting timed drills of various combinations of letters or words. The difference is that on her home computer, the timing is done by the computer, and speed and accuracy are reported automatically after each short drill. Carla can watch her typing skill improve, and she can see exactly what she's having trouble with at any point. She also plays a game called Type Attack, where letters advance down the screen as do aliens in a Space Invaders game. She has to type the letters before they reach the bottom in order to win. The game is so motivating that she works on drill more than the average typing student would. Carla's parents feel that she is learning far more from her work at home than she would in a once-a-week class at the local community center or from a self-study book, the other options they considered. In addition, she has the pride of accomplishing something on her own and acquiring a skill most of her peers don't have.

Drawing on the Computer

Melissa is a child who loves to draw. She is very talented and does excellent drawings for an eight-year-old. Unfortunately, from the point of view of her parents, Melissa spends too much time drawing and not enough working at her school subjects. Her teacher has found that instead of completing a test, Melissa will draw pictures on her test paper, and she draws instead of listening in class. When Melissa's parents bought her a computer, they bought one with the Logo language, which, among other things, allows young children to do drawings on the screen. They thought that the ability to draw would attract her to the computer, and they hoped that in time they would be able to interest her in the other things she could do on the computer as well.

Melissa naturally was eager to draw on the computer, and she plunged ahead in learning Logo in a class her parents enrolled her in. She soon found that to produce drawings with Logo, she had to do some arithmetic to calculate lengths of lines and directions of angles. While this is the sort of thing she pays no attention to in school, she was willing to do it for this new hobby. Melissa's parents found themselves answering her questions about arithmetic, lines, and angles and watching with surprise as she worked out routines involving mathematical reasoning that is rather sophisticated for her age. They hope that she will pay more attention to arithmetic in school as well, now that she can see a relevance to the subject matter.

Whether Melissa's art will improve through her work with Logo remains to be seen. She still finds it easier to achieve the effects she wants with paper and crayon. Her parents will probably buy other hardware and software that will make it possible for her to draw freehand and see the results on the computer screen. But for now, they are happy to see that one of her school subjects has become meaningful to her.

Building Computer Hardware

Sarah is a teenager who became interested in computers by playing games on them. When her parents decided to buy her a computer, they picked one that came in kit form so she could put it together herself. Her father felt that she would understand more about computers if she saw how they worked inside, instead of thinking that it is all rather magical, as many people do. So Sarah and her father worked together to solder the various components of the computer, following the plan that came in the kit. Sarah found the whole process very easy, and now feels electronics are not beyond her understanding or ability.

Mark is a teenager with a real interest in computers and electronics. He has a rather sophisticated home computer and decided to try out his electronic skills by building a "game paddle" for it. A game paddle is a device that he can use to play video games. When he turns the dial on the paddle, the figure he's controlling will move on the screen. Mark did all the work of designing the game paddle himself, deciding how to lay out the electronic system. Even though the device is rather simple, producing it required Mark to put into practice concepts and methods that he had previously only read about.

Activities for Preschoolers

Three-year-old Steven plays games on the family computer with the help of his mother, father, or older brother. He enjoys the experience, and his hand-eye coordination has improved noticeably while he is learning to think of the computer as an ordinary part of his life. The computer also provides a way for all of the family members to work at an activity together, despite their age differences.

Amy is a four-year-old who plays educational games on the computer. She plays a game where she sees a number on the screen and matches it to a number on the keyboard. In another, she counts blocks shown on the screen and types the correct number. She'll move on to adding and subtracting blocks. Amy isn't learning just from the computer. She works on these and other skills at her nursery school, but the computer gives her a chance to practice at home. As is true for Steven, Amy also enjoys having a chance to use the computer as her older brother and sister do.

Computers and the Community

A group of ninth-graders in a small college town in New York State made a deal with the high school computer teacher. Because they were not eligible to take the school's computer course until the next year, he offered them the chance to take a special after-school course in programming if they would, in turn, agree to tutor a group of senior citizens and teach them programming. The students would learn a concept, practice with it in one class, and then teach it to *their* pupils in a second class. The students were confident of their ability to do this, while a group of people from a local senior-citizen's club were interested in finding out more about computers, and the project began.

Most of these young high-school students learned programming fairly easily. They found it much harder to teach it to the adults. At first, they would get very frustrated when they had to explain an idea two or three times to someone. Most children don't realize the difficulties of communicating new ideas to other people and don't realize that the things they take for granted may not be part of another person's knowledge. The students had to come to terms with these difficulties and begin to think about how they could make themselves clear to other people.

Some of the adults also did quite well in programming; others found that computers were not interesting to them and dropped out of the class. By the end of the year, the numbers of adults had decreased so that the students were working on a one-to-one basis with the same adults each week, and they came to know them well and to like them. So, for these children, computers became an opportunity to have an unusual amount of contact with people they wouldn't ordinarily see much of, and an opportunity to learn what it's like to help someone else acquire a new skill.

WHAT CHILDREN GAIN FROM COMPUTERS

Parents buy computers for their children for many reasons. After all, computers support a range of activities, both familiar, like arithmetic drill, and new, like video games, that weren't possible without computers. In the examples we've just discussed, computers have helped in writing, music, art, and a variety of other areas.

However, as we've seen, it's not always possible to say what the results or the benefits of a computer will be. There is often serendipity in working with computers that causes the results to be unpredictable. Sometimes a child will use a computer for a purpose that's totally unexpected by her parents. Sometimes, as in some of our examples, the computer activity produces growth in an unexpected way. Once you buy a computer for your child, you hope that she will truly make that computer her own and use it in ways that make sense to her.

HOW CHILDREN VIEW COMPUTERS

There's a feeling today that children and computers are a perfect match, that all children take to computers naturally and easily. We've often heard people comment on how quickly their children learned to use the family computer, how they didn't have any fear of technology to overcome, and how they seemed to be able to adapt their thinking to computers. It's true that the excitement of computers seems to capture most children.

But not all children become computer whiz-kids. Many children have a take-it-or-leave-it attitude toward computers. They may study computers in one course at school and enjoy the work, but have no desire to continue. If their parents buy them a computer, that's fine, but they don't plan to use it very much. Other children dislike computers. Perhaps they're afraid to try something new because they may fail. Perhaps they don't know much about computers and don't see any benefit in having a computer.

As in many other activities, there is a range in the degree of interest that children have in computers. Like adults, children tend to be most interested in computers when they find that the computer meets a need that they have or in some personal way catches their imagination.

Probably the most exciting thing about computers for many children is the video games they can play. The computer graphics, animation, sound, and action are very stimulating for many, if not most, children. Video arcade games like Space Invaders or Pac-Man are a part of our children's culture and they associate video games with computers. Trying to write a video game or creating a graphic on the screen similar to something they've seen in an arcade game is one of the most common things children do when they start to program a computer. In particular, children who don't have a computer and who haven't had much exposure to computers at school think that game playing is one of the most important things computers can do for them.

As children become more exposed to computers, their attitudes toward computers often change. Many tire of video games and of repeating the same type of activity over and over. They want to get away from the passive role of game-player and make the computer do something they are interested in. They begin to seek out programming experiences, using BASIC or Logo; they look for adventure games and simulation exercises that require thought and analysis; or they try out educational programs that let them explore a new skill.

Children feel that computers are part of the future, and they want to learn about computers to be part of that future. One fourteen-year-old, who was part of a panel of young computer users at a computer conference, said, "If people don't learn computers, they won't be able to go anywhere in the year 2001." Other children express the same idea. Using computers will help you "get ahead," while not learning about computers will mean you're "left behind." Their parents probably agree, because many parents say similar things.

What kinds of needs do computers satisfy for children? Many children talk about how knowledge of computers will help them get a job later on. It seems rather surprising that even rather young children, such as a group of ten-year-old Girl Scouts that we spoke to at a computer exhibition, are thinking about how they will find work when they grow up, but we've found it to be a very common concern. Perhaps this is a result of recent economic troubles. Some of these children probably imagine themselves working at a traditional computer job like programming, but others have absorbed the idea that every job in the future will involve some interaction with computers.

Many children have what was to us a rather unexpected knowledge of what computers can do for them. Both children who have computers at home and those who don't will speak about some very specific tasks they think a computer can do. (Often, they're clearer in their perceptions of this than are adults.) One nine-year-old spoke of being able to use a computer to look up a year in the past to find out what happened at that time when she is writing a history report. This kind of activity would be possible if she had access to a history or encyclopedia database via a home computer and "modem." (We'll describe *modems* in Chapter 3.) Other children tell us that they think computers can help them in science, in math, and in spelling (either by finding all their errors with a word processor or by teaching them to spell).

Some children also have an awareness of trends in the computer field. The same nine-year-old girl predicted that computers would become more complex in what they can do and at the same time be easier to use, which is very likely true.

How do children feel about using computers? Many children find being in control of a computer very rewarding. One boy spoke of knowing things that his parents didn't know and said,

"I love doing things adults can't do." Knowing how to use a computer gives them a sense of power and accomplishment that makes them feel more adult.

In children's thoughts about computers there is often an element of magic. Some computer teachers have said that children begin to think of the computer as a person, one that will respond to their instructions and with whom they have a relationship. Many seem to feel that the computer is a magician, able to grant their wishes. Indeed, there is something a little magical to many adults too about a machine that can do such complex tasks and appear to understand so much.

Working at a computer is very compelling for many children. They become absorbed in what they're doing, whether it's a video game or their own computer program. A computer provides a variety of experiences all at once—visual, auditory, mental, and imaginative. Children respond to the challenge of bettering their own performance in a video game, of increasing their skills in an educational program, and of creating a computer program and making it work.

Using a computer does not replace all other activities in a child's life. Children who enjoy working with computers also continue to read, play sports, watch TV, etc. Although there may be times when a child appears obsessed with this new hobby, most children maintain a balance. Children themselves recognize that there is more to life than computers. One child said that he likes to read more than he likes to play with computers because he finds out more from books.

THE AGE QUESTION

Many parents are concerned about what is the best age for a child to start using computers. They wonder whether their child is old enough for computers or whether she is so old that she's already missed the boat. The whole issue of how old children should be when they get a computer is complicated by ads for computers that show a boy so young that he has to sit on his father's lap to use the computer, and a girl getting a computer for a fifth-birthday present. The implication is that these parents are doing the right thing, while other parents are not giving their very young children the right start in life. And of course, if a preschooler needs a computer, then an older child *absolutely* must have one.

Nonsense. We think that computers are beneficial for children, but we don't believe that every child must have one or that there is one "right" age to make that purchase. In this section we'll describe the ways children of different ages can use the computer. Later in the book, in Chapter 4, we'll describe specific computer activities in more detail. From this information you, as a parent, should be able to decide whether it makes sense to buy a computer now for your child, to wait to buy one later, or not to buy one at all in the foreseeable future. The decision should be comparable to decisions you make about other areas of your child's life, such as whether she should start piano lessons or whether she should go to camp. Base your decision on whether you think your child is ready for a computer and whether you think the results will be positive ones.

Preschool

The biggest area of controversy about computers is probably with regard to children of preschool age, from two and one-half to five years old. On one side are parents who think that if their child doesn't have a computer both in nursery school and at home, she'll be left behind. On the other side are parents who are concerned that their children not take time away from more traditional toys and from other important learning activities.

With a preschool child, it's important to keep a sense of proportion. While computers can be educational, for children of this age many other activities such as playing with sand, coloring, "reading" picture books, and playing with their peers are educational too. Nursery school teachers who have computers in their classrooms feel very strongly that children can benefit from computers, but that they shouldn't use them to the exclusion of everything else or even for a very large portion of the time.

If you decide to have your preschooler get some exposure to computers, she'll be using the computer to play learning games for preschool skills like alphabet recognition, counting, color matching, and shape matching. Several companies publish software designed for young children. Most of it has some educational content, but the software is designed to be fun to use as well.

She might do some drawing on the screen by moving a "joystick," or play with computer music using a very simple piece of software designed for young children. She might also play some computer video games, although these tend to be designed for older children. Most likely, you or your child's older brother or sister will have to sit with her while she's working at the computer, especially as she learns how to play any game. She'll probably work for only a few minutes (perhaps up to ten minutes) at a time on the computer, because attention spans tend to be very short in preschoolers.

For very young children, the context of computer use can be as important as the activity itself. One mother reported that her child benefited as much from the fact that he was regularly getting her direct, consistent attention and time when they did learning games on the computer, as he did from using the computer itself. They were both involved with the computer and interacting a great deal. Similarly, after dinner several times a week, when the father and older brother would join them in video games for half an hour or so, the younger child felt included as a participant in an activity the whole family was enjoying together.

Early Elementary School

A child in first to third grade can do more with a computer than can a preschooler. As she learns to read, she will be able to read simple instructions on the screen, which makes it much easier to work with computer software. There are a variety of simple-to-use educational computer games for children this age, that help improve such fundamental skills as addition and subtraction and reading. Other software will let her draw on the screen, make music, and play games that teach logic skills. A child this age will also begin to develop skill at video games on the computer.

Many children of these ages learn computer programming in school, in a computer school or camp, or at home with their parents. Typically, the children learn the Logo computer language, and use it to create drawings on the computer screen.

These children are usually not capable of doing very sophisticated programming, but they make a start in learning what a computer language is and how to use it. They also learn how to divide tasks into parts for the computer, look for parts that repeat, and find and correct errors.

Upper Elementary School and Junior High

Children from fourth grade through junior high are developing the cognitive skills and the sophistication to do some fairly elaborate things with the computer. This is an age range in which computer use can really blossom.

The typical child is ready by junior high to learn programming, and may do well at it even earlier. She can master some very sophisticated programming techniques. She'll use the computer for educational games covering a wide range of skills in math, science, spelling, reading, etc. She may become a champion computer-video-game player as well.

At this age your child can use the computer for creative work in art, music, and writing. Your child can explore techniques of music composition, story writing, computer graphics, etc. The computer will encourage her to apply planning skills to her own creative ideas and to appreciate the importance of form in art.

Many junior-high children will develop their own special computer hobbies and projects. They may join computer clubs or have a group of friends who all have computers, and they'll share knowledge of the technology with each other. Parents are often surprised at the sophistication of the computer activities these children engage in.

High School and College

A young adult of high-school or college age will still use the computer for educational purposes. She may work through a simulated science experiment on the computer, use the computer to practice SAT test-taking skills, or learn a foreign language via the computer, but she'll play far fewer educational games than younger children. The main educational use of the computer will be as a tool to help in computations for science or advanced math or as a word processor for writing papers.

Computer programming is probably the major computer interest for students in high school and college. Students will study one or more computer languages and use a wide variety of computer "peripherals" (accessories). And like their younger siblings, they may continue to play the computer video games that seem to have such universal popularity.

Some young adults of these ages will use computers in very sophisticated ways. High-school and college students can develop a high level of skill in computer art, music, and programming. Many actually become professionals, earning money for their skills. They may also begin to use the computer for the same things adults use it for. A business-school student may use a computer as a financial tool, and an engineering student may use it for mathematical calculations.

HOW YOUR CHILD FITS INTO THE PICTURE

You've now read about a number of things children can do with a computer and about the kinds of good things that can result from its use. You're probably beginning to see some of the ways your child might use a computer, but you may be wondering just how all these exciting activities are done on a computer. In the chapters that follow, we'll try to clear up these points and help you to pick out the computer that will be best for your child.

As you begin the process of exploring what your child can do with a computer, you'll need to be familiar with some of the terms and concepts that are part of the computer field. In the next chapter, you'll have a chance to learn this basic information.

CHAPTER 3

A Crash Course in Computers

Now that you know something about what children can do with computers, it's time to learn the essentials of the computer itself. In this chapter we'll explain the crucial computer terms and concepts that you will encounter over and over in selecting a computer. Armed with this knowledge, you can talk with salespeople, read ads, understand the hardware discussions in the rest of this book, relate hardware (equipment) and software (programs) to actual computer tasks we describe later, and make an intelligent choice of a computer for your child.

Parents vary in their level of understanding of, and exposure to, the computer field. Even people with years of experience on large computer systems often draw a blank when it comes to personal computers (or microcomputers, as they are often called). For these reasons, we have written about computers in such a way that each section should be understandable to the newcomer.

You may find it difficult to absorb all the information in this chapter at once. If you like, you can read part of the chapter now and then return to it as you read later chapters and discover that you need to understand a specific concept or term.

Rather than abstractly describing computers and how they work, this chapter will describe and explain important computer features by showing how each feature is used in an activity that a child might engage in on the computer. To do this, we'll look at two different activities: a *math drill* on the computer and a *database* system that a child uses.

The math drill is one used by eight-year-old Scott to improve his knowledge of multiplication tables. Scott sees "2 × 2" on the screen attached to his Atari computer. The direction "Type the answer" is at the bottom of the screen. A drawing of a monkey standing next to a palm tree is at the right side of the screen. When Scott types "4" on the keyboard, a message like "That's right!" appears at the bottom of the screen. Then the monkey climbs part way up the tree. Each time Scott solves a problem correctly, the monkey climbs farther up the tree until eventually he reaches the coconut at the top and Scott has "won" the game.

Twelve-year-old Lisa uses a database system on her IBM computer. Her hobby is identifying different types of rocks. The database system allows her to store and sort through information on rocks. The screen is set up so that it looks rather like a filecard with headings on different lines. Lisa decides what each heading should be on this basic card. She has headings for the color of the rock, mineral content, and other important features. As she reads about different kinds of rocks, she enters her information on the file cards. Later she can use the database when she's trying to identify a rock that she has found. If the rock is white and shiny, she can ask the database to give her all the rocks that fit that description. One at a time, the computer will show her each card that matches. She can check the other information on each card to see whether this matches her sample.

SOME FACTS ABOUT COMPUTERS

When you look at a computer, you are actually looking at a group of different devices hooked together to perform as a computer. The most important part of the computer, the "brain" of the computer where it performs all its calculations and stores information, is hidden. This collection of silicon chips

—one of which is called the *central processing unit* (CPU), and others that are its accompanying memory and special-purpose units—is inside the case. (Although we call the CPU the "brain" of the computer, the intelligence of the system really lies in the software. The CPU is only capable of getting one instruction at a time from the software and carrying out that instruction.) Often the CPU and its accompanying chips are behind or underneath the *keyboard,* which is the part of the computer that looks like a typewriter.

Attached to the central processing unit and keyboard is the *screen* on which you see text and graphics displayed. The computer will also have a *storage device,* where information and instructions are stored. This will be either a cassette recorder, cartridge player, or a disk drive. Generally speaking, all "input" devices (here, the keyboard), "output" devices (here, the screen), and storage devices are called *peripherals,* because they are attached to or surround the CPU. We'll talk about each of these parts and others in this chapter. *Figure 3–1* shows these parts and their relationships.

FIGURE *3–1* / **Basic Parts of a Computer System**

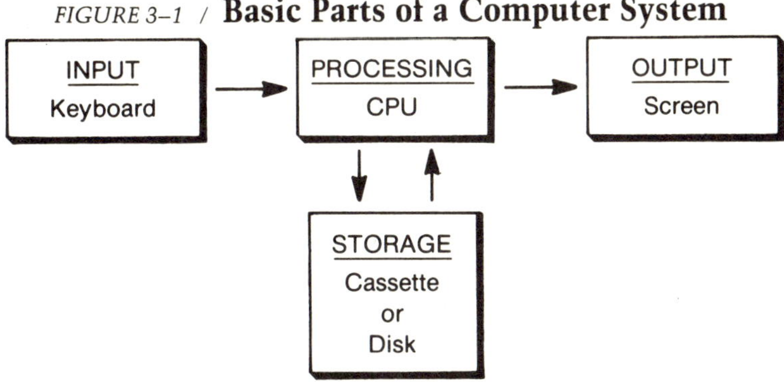

When people talk about computers, they often use the terms *hardware* and *software.* Computer hardware is the part of the computer we've just described, the tangible part of the computer. You can think of computer hardware as analogous to the components of a stereo system. A stereo is designed to play records; a computer too is designed to "play software." Computer software, sometimes referred to as a computer program, is the set of directions that cause the computer to carry out a task, whether that task is playing a video game or handling a database. You can think of software as analogous to the music on a record. Software is even recorded and sold on a disk or a tape; it is a recording of electronic information.

Unlike a record, which can be played on any stereo system, computer software is usually designed for use on only one computer. Atari programs don't play on IBM, for example. Popular programs are often "translated" for other computers, but may not be as effective with different graphics. People often buy computers in order to run a particular piece of software that works only on that computer. Some computers are designed to use software from other manufacturers' computers, either as a standard or extra-cost feature. For example, the Compaq runs IBM software; the Franklin runs Apple software; and the IBM can run certain Apple software if you buy a special "card" for the IBM from a third-party supplier.

WHAT YOU SEE ON THE SCREEN

Color

The first thing you notice on a computer that is actually in use, rather than sitting on the shelf in a computer store, is the screen. The screen is where the action is. If you were looking over Scott's shoulder during the math drill, for example, you would watch the numbers appear on the screen and the monkey climb the tree. The images would appear in color on Scott's color TV set, which has been hooked up to the computer. The computer sends TV broadcast signals through an antenna wire connected to the antenna terminals of the TV set.

If Scott did not have a color TV, he could use a black-and-white set and see the monkey and the problems in black and white. Scott has a choice of whether or not to use a color set because his computer can give either a color or black-and-white image. This is not true of every computer; all produce black-and-white signals, but some do not produce color or there's an extra charge for color capability. For Scott's math drill it's not essential to see color, but computer art does look better in color, and for some educational and many artistic applications color is essential. Color, then, is the first important computer feature.

Computer Fact 1: Some computers produce a color picture, some just black-and-white.

Scott's computer has a choice of sixteen colors, and each color can be used in sixteen different intensities, making many different shades of colors possible. Lisa's computer also has sixteen colors. Some computers have four, eight, or some other number of colors. But even when a computer has a large number of colors, all of these colors will not be available to you all of the time for all purposes. If color is important to you (for example, if you want to use a lot of graphics with your computer), check carefully into how color can be used on the computer you plan to buy.

Lisa does not use a TV set as her screen. A computer screen is sometimes a television set; sometimes it is a *monitor*. A monitor is a television-like screen that is not equipped to pick up TV broadcast signals. Instead, it gets an electronic video signal directly from the computer through a cable. Generally speaking, you get a sharper picture on a monitor than on a TV. Lisa's parents share the computer with Lisa and use it for word processing, so they want the sharpest picture possible. They use an amber monitor (the type on the screen is orange) instead of the other choices, black-and-white, green-and-black, or color, because amber is thought to cause the least eyestrain for normal eyes. Lisa's computer will work with either a monitor or a TV, but some computers will work only with a monitor, and some software works only with a monitor.

Computer Fact 2: Some computers and some software require a monitor; others can use a TV set.

Text

Scott reads directions that show up on his TV in lines of forty characters across. Lisa's filecards show up on the monitor in lines of eighty characters across. The fewer the characters across the screen, the wider each one can be; so Scott can easily read his directions. The more characters across, the narrower each one must be, but with more characters on a line, you see more information on the screen at one time. Lisa can put twice as much information on each filecard screen line because she has twice as many characters on a line as Scott. Some other computers have line lengths of 22, 32, 64, or 132 characters. Most systems that have 80 characters across allow you to switch to 40 characters for other software. Each has advantages for certain applications.

Besides the number of characters across, computers differ in the number of lines of text—usually 16 to 24—that can be seen on the screen. Common configurations are 40 or 80 characters across by 24 lines down; or 32 or 64 characters across by 16 lines down. Note that only a monitor can show 80 characters across and 24 lines down with clarity. A TV set is generally limited to 40 characters by 24 lines to obtain reasonable clarity.

Computer Fact 3: Computers differ in the number of characters across and in the number of lines of text down that they can display on the screen.

Figure 3–2 compares the text screen dimensions of several typical computers. In the charts in this chapter we'll show a feature, such as the number of characters displayed, for a representative group of four or five computers. The computers indicated on each chart were chosen to give you an idea of the range of typical values that these features can take on and the degree of differences that exist in capability among different computers. In Chapter 5, we refer you to more extensive charts in Appendix B, showing how each of a larger number of computers compare on these features. The charts in Chapter 3 will help you become acquainted with computers; those in Appendix B will help you select one to buy.

Graphics

When Scott looks at the monkey on his computer screen, he is looking at graphics, not text. *Graphics* are pictures, shapes, lines, or anything that is not letters, numbers, special symbols, or punctuation. Graphics make educational software and

FIGURE 3–2 / **Comparison of Text-Screen Layouts**

Computer	Text Dimensions (Columns Across by Rows Down)	Comments
COMMODORE VIC20	22x23	
RADIO SHACK COLOR COM-PUTER 2	32x16	50 or more columns available with software from other suppliers
COLECO ADAM	36x24	80-column option to be available in future
APPLE IIe	40x24	80x24 available with optional board
IBM PCjr	40x25 (entry model) 80x25 (expanded model)	
KAYPRO II	80x24	Portable computer Built-in 9-inch screen

games more exciting and often more meaningful. All computer graphics have to be made up of building blocks called elements or *pixels* (picture elements). The screen is divided into a grid, like graph paper. Each square in the grid is an element on the screen. The elements can be black or white or they can be in a color. A graphic with a larger number of elements, which more finely divide the screen, has higher "resolution." High-resolution pictures are more realistic than low-resolution pictures.

Scott's computer has a number of element patterns available. The one that his software uses is 160 across by 80 down although his computer is capable of displaying 320 across by 192 down at its highest resolution. Both of these densities of elements are considered high resolution. Lisa's computer has a pattern of approximately 320 by 200, also high resolution. The monkey that Scott sees looks almost as well drawn as a monkey in a cartoon, but it would look better with the highest resolution setting of his or Lisa's computer or with a still higher resolution. In contrast, a broadcast television picture has a resolution in the range of about 320 by 480.

Scott's computer and most other computers also can show *low-resolution graphics,* which on his computer are forty by forty-eight, so each element is larger. The number of elements also varies in low resolution. Low-resolution graphics produce much cruder shapes, but also take less memory to produce than high-resolution graphics (we'll talk about memory later). Low-resolution graphics are sometimes preferable because

FIGURE 3–3 / **Comparison of Low-
and High-Resolution Graphics**

A figure in low-resolution

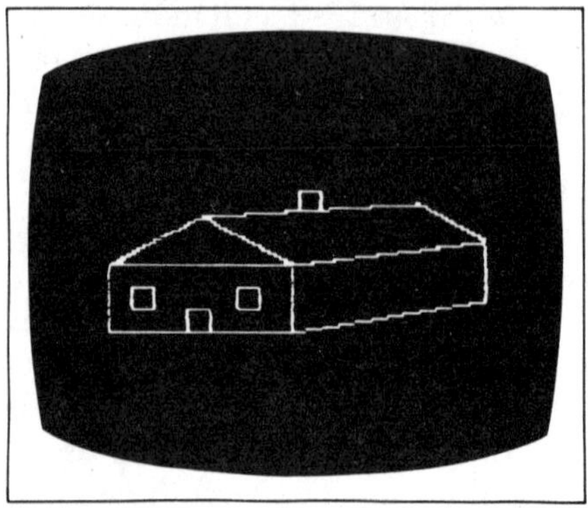

A figure in high-resolution

they're easier for a novice to use, and often allow more colors to be used.

The pictures in *Figure 3–3* show a house drawn at different resolutions.

The resolution of computer graphics is getting better and better. Resolutions of 600, 800, or even 1000 elements across are available on better personal computers.

Computer Fact 4: The resolution of different computer graphics varies. The higher the resolution, the clearer the graphics, but the more memory required to do the graphics.

Figure 3–4 shows the high-resolution capabilities of some typical systems.

FIGURE 3–4 / **High-Resolution Graphics Capabilities**

Computer	Highest Resolution	Comments
RADIO SHACK COLOR COMPUTER 2	256x192 (color)	
APPLE IIe	280x192 (b&w)	140x192 in color
ATARI 600XL	320x192 (color)	
IBM PC	640x200 (b&w)	320x200 in color
IBM PCjr	640x200 (color)	
NEC APC	640x475 (color)	

Figure 3–5 shows the number of colors available at different resolutions for a range of systems.

The monkey in Scott's program is animated; that is, it appears to move. This is accomplished by drawing the monkey in several different poses, arms up, arms down, etc., each of which looks like a different stage of climbing, and then flashing these pictures on the screen in rapid succession. It's a process similar to drawing an animated cartoon. All computers

FIGURE 3–5 / **Number of Colors Available**

Computer	Total Colors Possible	Number of Colors That Can Be Used at One Time in High Resolution
RADIO SHACK COLOR COMPUTER 2	9	2 colors at resolution 256x192 4 colors at resolution 128x192
APPLE IIe	16	6 colors at 140x192
COMMODORE 64	16	16 colors at 320x200 but only 4 colors in each 8x8 region
IBM PCjr	16	4 colors at 640x200 16 colors at 320x200
ATARI	256	2 colors at 320x192 4 colors at 160x192 8 colors at 160x96 16 intensities of 16 basic colors makes 256 possible shadings to choose from

with graphics can animate to some extent, but the animation is better on some computers than others. There is also a wide variation in how easy it is for the programmer to animate on different computers.

Computer Fact 5: Graphics and animation are not equally good on different computers. They are not equally easy to use either, and there is no strong relationship between quality of graphics and ease of use.

Scott programs computer graphics himself, but he doesn't use either the high- or low-resolution graphics on his computer. His computer has another common kind of graphics as well, *character-set graphics*. In character-set graphics, the computer gives you a set of building-block shapes with which to create a picture. Sometimes there are circles, curves, squares, half squares, and so forth, each the size of a letter on the screen. (On other computers, the graphics are simply patterns of small squares.) Using these, Scott is able to construct pictures. Often it is easier to work with these character-set graphics than the other kinds; it depends on the task. Some computers have only character-set graphics.

Computer Fact 6: Some computers have character-set graphics in addition to, or instead of, high- or low-resolution graphics.

Figure 3–6 shows two examples of character-set graphics. One includes diagonal elements and is used here to draw a helicopter. The other has only right-angle elements and is used to draw a house.

FIGURE 3–6 / **Drawings Done with Two Different Types of Character-set Graphics**

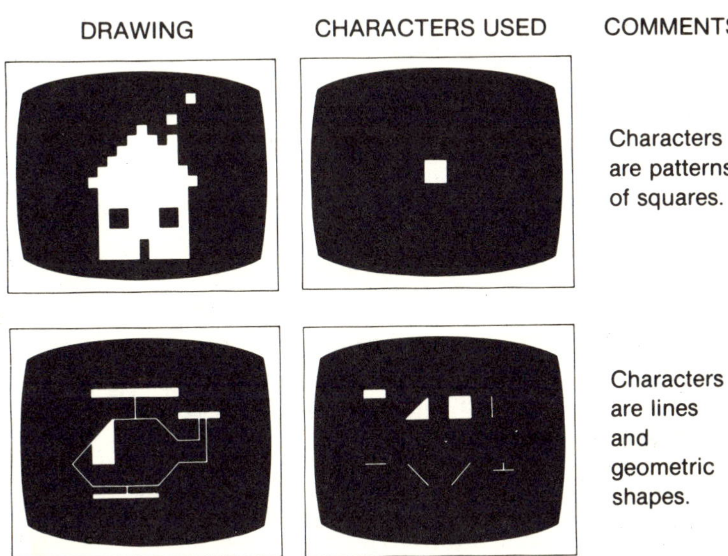

You may have heard of *turtle graphics*, which are often part of the Logo language. These are high-resolution graphics, but the methods used to create them are different. We'll discuss these in more detail in Chapter 5.

HOW YOU COMMUNICATE WITH THE COMPUTER

Keyboards

Both Scott and Lisa communicate their commands and responses to the computer by typing on the keyboard. The keys are laid out like a typical typewriter keyboard with the letters "QWERTYUIOP" on the top row, etc. A variety of different keyboards are available on computers. They vary from a small keyboard that you can use with one finger, to keyboards with calculator-type, rectangular or square keys that are not quite as big or comfortable to use as normal full-size typewriter keys (we will refer to these as "small-size keys" even though they are not tiny), to keyboards that feel as good as, or better than, an electric typewriter.

Keyboards also vary in availability and arrangement of special keys, such as arrows and "function keys" and also so-called "programmable function keys," where the use of the special key changes for each program. (By contrast, an ordinary function key has a fixed purpose that is marked on it, such as "print" or "insert.") There are differences in keyboard layout and spacing that affect the ease of use of the keyboard as well.

Figure 3–7 characterizes the keyboard capabilities of a typical group of systems.

Computer Fact 7: Keyboards vary in quality from those on which it is impossible to touch-type to those that are as good as, or better than, an electric typewriter.

The trend now is for keyboards to become increasingly versatile. The following kinds of features are emerging.

More function keys clearly marked for special tasks such as "print" or "delete" or "paste."
Detachable keyboards connected to the computer by cables

FIGURE 3–7 / **Keyboard Capabilities***

Computer	Types of Keys	User-Assigned Function Keys	Comments
RADIO SHACK MC-10	Small-size keys	0	Small keyboard Has special keys for entering BASIC commands Keys not suitable for touch-typing
IBM PCjr	Small-size keys	0**	Long narrow keys Cordless keyboard Keys not good for touch-typing
COLECO ADAM	Full-size, type-writer keys	6	Detachable keyboard, with cord
COMMODORE 64, COMMODORE VIC20	Full-size, typewriter keys	8	4 function keys used with and without shift
IBM PC	Full-size, typewriter keys	10	Detachable keyboard, with cord Separate number pad

* All have typewriter layout (QWERTY).

** But the values and uses of all keys can be reassigned by the software, and cardboard templates printed with new letter assignments appearing next to the keys can be fitted onto the keyboard. Because of this feature, any key can become a function key, and the order of the keys can be changed (for example, from "QWERTY" to alphabetical, for younger children).

---

   or cordless keyboards (using infrared signals as do TV remote controls).

Keyboards designed with shapes that curve over your lap or knees. (These aren't available yet for personal computers.)

Alternative keyboards, sold by third-party manufacturers, for use with popular computers. These include extra keys for single-stroke shortcuts or rearranged keyboards that are easier to use. These special keyboards may have particular advantages for children with physical or learning disabilities.

Joysticks

You've probably seen video arcade games where there is no keyboard at all. The player sends instructions on how to move by using a joystick or ball. Many computer video games also work with a joystick, ball, or paddle. All three can indicate the direction in which you want to move. The ball is a kind of large ball bearing that is rolled to indicate direction; a paddle has a dial that you turn; a joystick has a signal button as well as a handle that you push or pull in the direction you want to move. Scott hooks a joystick to his computer when he wants to play Pac-Man. Some educational programs, especially those for young children, use a joystick instead of the keyboard. Joysticks are particularly useful for preschool children, because the children aren't familiar with keyboards and letters. Joysticks or other special devices can be very useful for children with motor impairments as well.

Most computers, but not all, allow a joystick, paddle, etc., to be hooked up to them. However, not all software can be used with a joystick. The software has to be designed to accept information from the joystick or paddle.

> **Computer Fact 8: Joysticks and other devices can be used instead of a keyboard in some games and educational programs, but not all software will work with a joystick. Joysticks give the child direct control over movement on the screen and are especially good for drawing or pointing tasks.**

Graphics Tablets

Children and adults who do artwork on the computer often use another kind of communication device, a *graphics tablet*. There are a number of different tablets on the market, ranging in price from $100 to $600, but they all work more or less like this: The tablet, which looks like a slate, lies flat next to the computer. As you draw on the tablet with a special "pen," you see the lines you draw on the computer screen, rather than on the tablet.[1] You can color shapes by running your pen across them as you would a crayon, or, on many tablets, you can command the computer to fill in a shape with color. Tablets vary in ease of use and in the quality of the picture you get. Most often, you need some special software to use the tablet, and some of that software lets you do things like move parts of your drawing around the screen, straighten out lines, enlarge an area for better viewing while changing small details, and add text to your drawing. Some tablets come with the necessary software.

Computer Fact 9: Graphics tablets make art on the computer better and easier to do by allowing you to draw directly onto the screen.

Lightpens and Touch Screens

It is sometimes difficult for young children to use keyboards to indicate their commands and answers to a computer. Children are not ordinarily familiar with the layout of the keyboard, and can spend a great deal of time hunting for the letters to make up their responses. (Typing should probably be taught earlier in school than it is now, to help students use computers.) There are some other devices that can help out until a student learns to type or aid a student with motor impairments who can't manage typing. Such devices include *lightpens*, which allow the child to touch an answer directly on the screen. For example, the screen might have a question with three answer choices, A, B, and C. The child could touch the C with the lightpen; the computer would then register the answer and reply whether or not it is right. Lightpens are available for many computers. They vary considerably in quality and ease of use.

Touch screens are available for some computers. With a touch screen, the child touches a choice on the screen with a

---

[1] Technically, the tablet is known as a *digitizer* where X–Y coordinates are recorded and transmitted wherever the pen touches.

finger instead of a lightpen. For young children or motor impaired children, it is easier to point with a finger (or in the case of severely impaired children, with a mouthstick) than a lightpen. And for everyone, touching the screen gives the feeling of directly commanding the computer. Touch screens can be used anytime a lightpen can be used.

Computer Fact 10: Lightpens and touch screens make communicating with the computer easier and more direct.

Other ways of communicating with the computer are available for disabled children and adults. Mouthsticks, special switches (such as those attached to foot pedals or to articles of clothing, for example, the brim of a cap), voice recognition devices, etc. can be used. Even eye-tracking devices have been used with computers. Sometimes they call for modification of the computer or require special software.

Mice and Turtles

A *mouse* is a small, highly movable ball, covered on top by a case with one or more control buttons on it. A mouse is used to move the cursor—the blinking light, solid block, or underline that shows where you are on the screen. Put it on a tabletop, or your sleeve, if you wish, and roll it to the left or right to make the cursor go to the left or right on the screen. When the screen shows a group of graphic symbols, each of which is a different choice of something to do, you move the mouse, causing the cursor to go to your choice, push the button, and the computer detects the choice. You can also use the mouse to "drag" figures or blocks of text from one part of the screen to another.

The mouse concept was developed and introduced by Xerox a number of years ago for use in office work-stations and experimental educational systems. Apple Computer made the mouse the centerpiece of its original $10,000 Lisa office system and more recently its $2500 Macintosh system, which a number of universities are buying for their students. The mouse concept is gradually being adapted by a number of other computer companies to provide an additional source of communication to the computer.

Turtles are the exact reverse of mice. You move mice around to give information and directions to the computer. With a turtle, you use the keyboard and software commands to make the turtle move around. Sometimes the turtle is a mechanical creature attached to the computer, sometimes it is a shape on the screen.

Computer Fact 11: The mouse device allows you to make choices and issue commands to the computer without touching the keyboard or screen.

WHAT YOU HEAR FROM THE COMPUTER

When Scott uses the math-drill program, he hears sounds each time the monkey climbs farther up the tree. The sounds are like those coming from an arcade game. This is one example of sound from the computer. Other sounds from the computer include speech and music.

Bleeps, pings, rat-a-tats, and other arcade sounds can be produced by many personal computers and can add a lot to video games. The noises are made by speakers within the computer itself or by impulses sent by the computer to the TV set speaker. Essentially, the computer plays one or a series of musical notes but distorts each note to make the desired sound. A surprising range of noises can be made this way.

Computers that make sounds by distorting musical notes can play computer music as well. The quality and range of the music that can be produced by the computer varies. Some computers can play up to eight or more notes simultaneously. Each note is said to be played by a different "voice" or "channel," so you will see references to a computer with "four voices," for example. The four voices can play a chord with up to four notes or just one, two, or three notes at a time. The range of computer music from high to low notes varies too, with some computers playing more octaves than others. The quality of sound varies somewhat as well, but all computers produce a kind of "electronic" sound. Ease of use in music playing varies.

Figure 3–8 shows the musical capabilities of a range of systems.

Building from this base, it's possible to improve the music produced by many computers either through software or by buying attachments for the computer. The software packages make it easier to play music. Instead of writing your own program to instruct the computer to produce sounds, you use a piece of software that usually shows a musical staff, lets you specify each note to be played, and usually displays the notes

FIGURE 3–8 / **Music Capabilities**

Computer	Number of Voices	Number of Octaves	Comments
ATARI 800XL	4	3	Good for simple uses Music software packages available
APPLE IIe	1	9	Good for a range of uses, but only with proper accessories Special music boards, keyboards, and software packages available from other manufacturers
COMMODORE 64	3	9	Sophisticated and powerful, but not easy to use without special software Built-in ADSR generator (attack/decay and sustain/release control) Programmable filters Hi-fi capabilities
IBM PCjr	3	7	Good for simple uses at present A variety of music software packages and accessories is likely to emerge

on the staff for you. Anytime you like, you can hear what you've written. You can compose something original or transfer a piece of music to the computer from sheet music.

The most important difference in sound quality has to do with how the notes are created. Most computers use only simple "tone generators" to create a musical sound that lacks richness or complexity. By contrast, some computers use (or let you attach) a "music synthesizer," that produces complex sounds with tone color and dynamics like real musical instruments. A music synthesizer is an economical alternative to the very expensive synthesizers used by professional musicians, which are electronic circuits that do nothing but play music. (The young composer in the movie *Fame* used such a device.) These stand-alone devices often cost $10,000 or more for a professional piece of equipment, whereas a good-quality synthesizer accessory for a computer might cost only $1000 or $2000 (or even as little as $300 or less for a simple version), because it makes use of the Apple, Commodore, or some other computer instead of containing its own expensive special built-in computer. The synthesizer peripheral also gives greater flexibility for creating, altering, and storing music.

Synthesizers that attach to a personal computer give the computer the ability to produce a wider range of notes (more octaves) as well as the ability to mimic different instruments. All of these play through the amplifier and speakers of your stereo system. On the simpler of these synthesizers, you tell the computer what note to play and select the kind of instrument you want it to sound like from a choice of a few instruments. At the other end of the spectrum, there are synthesizers that allow you to play on a piano-like keyboard, vary the sound-wave form and characteristics to sound like any real or imaginary instrument, record your music on disk, add other tracks, simulate a group of instruments, and produce printed sheet music.

Some computers have the ability to produce speech because they have additional peripherals, chiefly a speech (or "voice") synthesizer, and some additional software. The synthesizer will produce something resembling human speech; the quality of the sound varies widely. All speech synthesizers combine sound elements to produce speech. Some combine small phonetic elements to make words, some combine syllables or words. Each technique has its advantages. In addition, some speech-synthesis software packages are "rule-based," meaning that they automatically transform (even though crudely) any text that appears on the screen into syllables and sounds for the synthesizer to speak.

While speech synthesis is in a fairly primitive state now, it does offer some advantages. A speech synthesizer can make it possible for a visually-impaired person to use a computer. There will be real advances in speech-synthesizer technology in the next few years, with the quality of sound improving greatly. Children will be able to experiment with synthesis to create speech to go with their own programs.

Computer Fact 12: Sound from the computer comes in the form of music, speech, or arcade-game sounds. To get speech or better music, you need extra peripherals or built-in, special capabilities.

Some computers are starting to build in these advanced capabilities as standard features. For example, the Atari 1450XLD includes a speech synthesizer and the Commodore 64 includes a music synthesizer.

HOW THE COMPUTER COMMUNICATES

Printers

The computer responds to Scott and Lisa by printing characters and graphics on the screen. It can also communicate far more widely. Two devices the computer can communicate with are *printers* and *modems*.

When Lisa wishes to have a copy of what she's entered into her database so that she can take it with her while looking for rocks, she gets a printed copy of her filecards from the printer attached to her computer. She does this by typing a command in her database program to tell the computer to print. It responds by asking on the screen if the printer is turned on. If she responds yes, the computer activates the printer by sending it information to print. Within a few minutes, Lisa has a computer print-out on a long perforated sheet that she can separate into standard 8½ × 11 inch pages.

Lisa's computer communicates with the printer through a cable. One end of the cable accepts information from the computer, the other end communicates it to the printer. Communications can be either *serial* or *parallel,* which refers to how the information codes travel. (Put simply, *serial* communication sends one piece of information at a time until the code for an entire character is received. *Parallel* sends the whole code at once, eight or more pieces of information, using one wire for each.) A typical *serial interface* between computer and printer is the "RS-232C" interface; a typical *parallel interface* is the "Centronics" interface, which goes to Centronics brand printers and many others. Parallel interfaces are more common. When you buy a computer and printer, it's important to be sure that the interface on the computer (or that you can add) matches the interface required by the printer.

Printers can be as complex to discuss as computers, but basically, the distinguishing features of different printers are speed, quality of the printed image on the page, price, type of paper they use, and the amount of noise they produce as they work.

A typical inexpensive printer, like Lisa's, uses *dot-matrix* technology to produce letters on the page. Each letter is made up of a pattern of dots placed very close together. Depending on how many dots are used to make up a letter and how close they are, the letter looks more or less like a typewriter's letters. Lisa's printer, with a dot matrix that is 7 dots by 9 dots, is very readable, but the lines that make up the letters are not solid as they are in typewriter type. Newer, more expensive printers offer 9 dots by 18 dots or even denser character matrices. The speed of dot-matrix printers varies widely. More expensive printers are usually much faster. Lisa's printer, which prints 50 characters per second, is acceptable in speed for her work, taking half a minute or so to print a full page. Other printers run at higher speeds such as 80, 120, 160, and even 200 or more characters per second. Prices for such higher speeds are coming down. Overall, in the dot-matrix category, low-priced printers (such as the Gemini 10X) cost around $100–$400, medium-priced printers (such as the Epson FX-80) around $400–$700, and higher-priced printers around $700–$2000.

The speed of a printer is increased by bidirectionality, the ability to print both forward and also backward, on the return trip, so no time is wasted.

Printers that are considered *letter quality* (that is, the characters they produce are solid like typewriter type) are generally more expensive. Typically, they use a *daisy wheel*, which is a flat round disk that whirls and strikes the page with the desired letter as the printer operates. A variation on the daisy wheel is the *thimble element*, or *shuttlecock*. It can be thought of as a flat daisy wheel with all the petals turned upward from the center like a badminton shuttlecock. It is highly reliable and is less subject to wear. The thimble element was popularized by NEC, a well-known Japanese computer manufacturer.

Letter-quality printers tend to be slower than the inexpensive dot-matrix printers. Speed is also a function of price in letter-quality printers. Low-cost products clustering around $400–$700 and sometimes lower, tend to run at about 12 to 14 characters per second, similar to an electric typewriter. Intermediate speeds are 20, 25, 35, and 45 cps. Currently, they sell for about $700–$2000, but prices are steadily dropping. The fastest common letter-quality printers, with speeds of 55 cps, often sell for $2000 or more.

Some newer personal computers are now being offered with a letter-quality printer as part of the computer package for a total price of about $700. These printers are generally noisier and less reliable than the older types of printers, but may be adequate for your situation.

Bear in mind that while you are printing, you generally cannot do other work on the computer, so waiting for a print-out can delay your work. For most children, this kind of interruption is not a problem. If you need it, however, a printer (or a computer) with a *print buffer* makes it possible to continue working on the computer while you are printing.

Some typewriters can be hooked up to a computer as a printer if you pay to add an "interface board." They are very slow, but you can use the typewriter as an ordinary typewriter when it's not hooked up to the computer, and this flexibility can be useful. Generally, however, unless you must have letter-quality print and can't afford it in a printer, you're better off with a reliable, fast, dot-matrix printer. You can buy a typewriter separately.

Some dot-matrix printers are now offering "near-letter-quality" printing by including a two-speed option. At the fast speed (around 160 cps), the printer produces ordinary "draft quality," but at the slow speed (around 40 or 50 cps), the printer produces a denser "correspondence quality" type that is dark and nearly solid. This might be a good choice for a parent who wants to share a computer and printer with a child and who wants to produce good-looking text for professional reports while having a fast printer speed for the child's activities (such as graphics) or for rough drafts.

The paper used by different printers varies. Some inexpensive printers require special heat-sensitive paper (used by "thermal" printers) or electrostatic paper (paper sensitive to electric charge). This paper can be expensive. Most printers use regular paper.

Sometimes the paper printers use is *fan-folded*. This is connected 8½ × 11 inch pieces of paper with holes punched along a perforated side margin. The printer pulls the paper through with pins that fit into the holes. The pin mechanism is called a *tractor feed*. Some printers allow the fan-fold paper, or a roll of paper, to be fed into the printer without a tractor, using platen pressure on the paper to pull it through, in the manner that paper is pulled through a typewriter. These printers are called *friction-feed* printers. Tractor feeding is more reliable, but you can feed a single sheet of paper, perhaps your personal stationery, through a friction-feed printer. Many printers allow you to choose either tractor or friction feed when you print.

Printers vary widely in the amount of noise they produce as they operate. In particular, many of the low-priced printers tend to be noisier than their high-priced counterparts. You should check to see that the noise level of the printer you buy will be acceptable to you. Some people complain that they can hear a noisy printer all over the house.

Figure 3–9 compares a group of printers for their characteristics in terms of print quality, speed, price, type of paper used, and paper-feed mechanisms.

Computer Fact 13: Printers vary greatly in interface, in speed, in print quality (dot matrix versus letter quality), in printing mechanisms and reliability, in type of paper used and how it's handled, and in special features such as buffering.

FIGURE 3–9 / **Printers**

(NOTE: This chart is intended to acquaint readers with the wide range of capabilities and styles of printers that are available. Many other printers could also be listed—for example, Juki, Silver-Reed, and Diablo.)

| | A. DOT-MATRIX | | |
Printer	Speed in Characters per Second	Number of Columns (Normal Mode)	Comments
Under $100:			
RADIO SHACK TP-10	30	32	Uses thermal paper Friction feed only; no tractor
$100–$200:			
IBM PCjr COMPACT PRINTER	50	80	Uses thermal paper Friction feed only, no tractor
$200–$400:			
GEMINI 10X	120	80	Tractor and friction feed
$400–$700:			
TRANSTAR 315	50	80	Prints color graphics Tractor and friction feed
EPSON FX–80	160	80	Includes foreign language alphabets Friction and tractor model available
OKIDATA MICROLINE 92	160	80	Two speeds available: one for drafts, one for near letter-quality Typefonts can be customized Friction and pin-feed (similar to tractor)

Over $700:

Printer			Comments
MANNESMAN TALLY MT160L	160	80	Two speeds available 160 columns with condensed print Very durable Friction and tractor feed
EPSON FX–100	100	132	Extra-wide carriage Friction and tractor feed
IBM PC COLOR PRINTER	200	132	Prints color graphics Three speeds available (35, 100, 200 cps) for improving text quality

<table>
<tr><td colspan="4" align="center">B. LETTER-QUALITY</td></tr>
<tr><td>Printer</td><td>Speed in Characters per Second</td><td>Print Mechanism</td><td>Comments</td></tr>
</table>

Under $400:

Printer	Speed in Characters per Second	Print Mechanism	Comments
COLECO ADAM PRINTER (included with computer)	10	Daisy wheel	Has both tractor and friction Daisy wheels can be switched to change print styles Somewhat loud
ATARI 1027	20	Tube	Cannot switch tubes to change print styles Relatively quiet Friction feed only

$400–$700:

Printer	Speed in Characters per Second	Print Mechanism	Comments
COMREX CR–2	13	Daisy wheel	Friction only, but tractor available as option
TRANSTAR 120	14	Daisy wheel	Friction only, but tractor available as option
NEC AUTHENTIC 15LQ	14	Daisy wheel	Durable Can use metal daisy wheels Friction and tractor

*FIGURE 3–9 / **Printers** (continued)*

B. LETTER-QUALITY			
Printer	**Speed in Characters per Second**	**Print Mechanism**	**Comments**

Over $700:

(All have friction- and tractor-feed)

Printer	Speed	Mechanism	Comments
NEC SPIN-WRITER 2050	20	Thimble	Specifically designed to take advantage of special capabilities of IBM PC
C.ITOH F-10 STAR-WRITER	40	Daisy wheel	
NEC SPIN-WRITER 3550	33	Thimble	Specifically designed to take advantage of special capabilities of IBM PC
C.ITOH PRINT-MASTER	55	Daisy wheel	

(NOTE: Letter-quality printers usually do not have the ability to print graphics.)

Printers also vary in a number of other characteristics: ability to print graphics or colors; special features such as underlining, boldface, italics, subscripts and superscripts; and special symbols such as foreign language characters and markings, mathematical symbols, and foreign currency symbols. These special features must also be available in the software package you are using in order for the printer to print them. And conversely, just because the software includes these features does not guarantee that the printer will, too. So, if your child needs to print graphics or produce elaborately formatted documents or to do work with foreign language materials or advanced scientific notation, then be sure to seek out these capabilities in *both* the software and the printer.

Finally, devices that use pens to draw lines (often in color) are called *plotters*.

Modems

Sometimes Eric uses his computer to send messages to a friend of his who also has a computer. To do this, Eric uses a modem. Modem stands for "modulator-demodulator." The modem is hooked to Eric's computer and also to a phone line through an ordinary phone jack. The modem converts information from Eric's computer to audio signals that can be transmitted along a phone line. Eric instructs the computer to tell the modem to dial a number and send a message along the phone line. At the other end of the connection is an electronic network system that receives Eric's message and holds it in an "electronic mailbox" for his friend. When Eric's friend also dials the network, he can instruct his computer to tell the modem to pick up any messages from the mailbox and display them on the screen.

Modems differ in the speed at which they transmit information. The rate is measured with a unit called a *baud;* 300 baud and 1200 baud are the standards. A modem at 1200 baud transmits information four times faster than at 300 baud and is more expensive, but it will fill the screen quickly rather than slowly.

The 300-baud modems cost about $100 to $200, or more, depending on whether they include such special features as automatic dialing and answering. The 1200-baud modems cost about $500 to $600, and are becoming more popular. As is the case with many computer peripherals, modem prices continue to fall.

With a modem you can call an electronic network as Eric does or dial another computer directly. (Some modems automatically answer calls that come in to the computer so no one has to be there to instruct the modem to receive a message.) Electronic networks offer a variety of services, including access to programs, stock quotes, newswires, information sources, and electronic bulletin boards of information. The networks usually charge by the minute for hook-up time.

If your child is going to use a modem for long stretches of time, be prepared to put in a second telephone line so that the computer use does not restrict your ability to make or receive ordinary phone calls.

In addition to national electronic networks, in many cities

and regions there are also local electronic bulletin boards, organized by computer clubs or by other interest groups. Using special software for such computers as Atari or Apple, your child can even create his own bulletin board as hundreds of young computer hobbyists have done.

Computer Fact 14: A modem allows your computer to communicate with other computers or with electronic networks.

HOW YOU STORE INFORMATION

Computer Memory

When Scott begins his math drill, he puts a cassette containing his math software into a cassette player connected by a cable to the computer. The player is a special one sold with his computer; some computers use any cassette player. Scott types a command to the computer, and the computer activates the cassette player and picks up the information from the tape. The math-drill program is now stored in the computer's "memory." The computer's memory is a section of hardware where the electronic impulses that make up the instructions for the program can be stored. In addition, other data used by or later generated by the program itself can be placed in memory for reference by the program. Once the program is in memory, Scott can start the math drill by instructing the computer to run the program. The program will remain in memory until the computer is turned off, when the program will be lost, or until another program is loaded. Scott will be able to use the program again only if he reloads the cassette.[2]

The memory that holds the math drill is *internal* memory because it is part of the computer. Computer memory is measured in "bytes." A byte holds a single character—a number or letter—in a program or in data. Computers need to store both programs and data like Lisa's filecards. The larger the number of bytes the computer has, the more data and program

---

[2] There are special types of memories in which programs and data are not lost when the power is turned off. The most common is CMOS memory, such as that used in the Radio Shack Model 100 portable computer. Another kind is *bubble memory*, such as that used in the Grid Systems Compass computer.

characters the computer can store at one time. Usually, people talk of "kilobytes" or "K." 1K equals roughly 1000 bytes.[3] So Scott's computer, which has 16K of memory, has about 16,000 bytes, or 16,000 characters in which to store a program.

Computer memory is ordinarily provided in multiples of 8K or 16K: 8K, 16K, 32K, 64K, 128K, 256K, etc. You can usually purchase additional memory for your computer if you need it, up to the maximum your computer can hold. Lisa's computer's memory has been expanded to 64K, which means she can store much larger programs than in the 16K minimum for her system. The capacity of a computer in kilobytes is important because you can't run a program that is larger than the amount of memory your computer has. Scott can't use programs that take more than 16K; Lisa can't use programs that require more than 64K.

Computer Fact 15: Computer memory is measured in kilobytes, which are about 1000 characters. Different software programs require different minimum sizes of memory.

Figure 3–10 compares the memory size and memory expandability of a group of systems.

The term *RAM* is often used to describe the memory available for *temporary* storage of programs like Scott's math-drill program. *RAM* stands for "random-access memory." The term that stands in contrast to RAM is *ROM*, for "read-only memory." ROM memory has information permanently stored in it, typically programs for processing the BASIC language, graphics, and other internal computer tasks, so these programs can come built right into the computer. *RAM* memory is always lost when the computer is turned off; *ROM* memory is never lost. The Coleco Adam word-processing program happens to be in ROM memory in that computer, so it is always available. *RAM* can be altered; *ROM* cannot be altered.

When Lisa works, she places a disk, a 5¼ inch Mylar "record," complete with its protective paper cover, inside the computer's disk drive. The computer reads the program from

---

[3] The exact number of bytes in a kilobyte is 1024; 2 multiplied by itself 10 times.

FIGURE 3–10 / **Memory Size and Expandability**

Computer	Standard Ram Memory	Maximum Ram Memory	Comments
RADIO SHACK MC–10	4K	20K	Memory adequate for learning BASIC and for use with modems and electronic networks; memory (and peripherals) too limited for many other functions
ATARI 600XL	16K	64K	Adequate memory (with 64K) for many tasks Atari 800XL comes with 64K as standard
COMMODORE 64	64K	64K	Adequate memory for many tasks
IBM PCjr (entry model)	64K	128K	Expansion memory permits very elaborate programs to be run IBM PCjr (expanded model) comes with 128K as standard
IBM PC	64K	640K	Large expansion memory good for running sophisticated programs and monitoring several tasks on screen at once Also potentially useful for working with long texts in word processing Extra memory can also be used to simulate a disk drive to increase program speed in some cases

("off") the disk, just as Scott's program was read from the cassette. The program now is in memory, and Lisa can create her filecards.

Lisa can store her filecards permanently by putting a blank disk in the disk drive and instructing the computer to "save" her filecards on the disk. The next time she can load these filecards back into the computer simply by instructing the computer to get the information from this disk. Cassettes and disks store information used by the computer outside the computer itself. RAM and ROM are *internal memory;* cassettes and disks are *external memory.* (Note: internal memory operates a great deal faster than external memory.) Just as the amount of storage space in the computer is limited, a cassette or disk has a finite amount of space, but it is usually much more space than is available in RAM.

The space on a storage disk is also measured in kilobytes. So Lisa's disks might hold 320K of information, part of which can be read into her 64K computer at one time. Another computer's disks might hold 140K or 90K. Scott's cassette has far less space. *Figure 3–11* gives the disk capacities for some typical systems.

Computer Fact 16: External storage holds programs and information permanently for retrieval by the computer at any time.

Cassette vs. Disk vs. Cartridge

The three most common types of external storage media are cassettes, disks, and cartridges. A cartridge plugs directly into a spot on the computer. It is actually a special computer memory chip with a program permanently stored on it. Because this is a permanent memory chip, it is an example of ROM memory, just like the built-in ROM we talked about earlier. When you plug the cartridge into the computer, it becomes an extension of internal ROM memory. (This also means that its instructions "load" into the computer much faster than from a disk or cassette, because internal memory operates faster than external memory.)

Scott can use cassettes or cartridges on his computer, or he can buy a disk drive and use disks. If he does buy a disk, he

FIGURE 3–11 / **Comparison of Storage Methods and Capacities**

Computer	Accepts Cartridges	Capacity Per Disk	Comments
SINCLAIR QL	Yes	No disk (but disk interface will be provided)	Adequate for learning BASIC and for small word processing and financial tasks Uses two high-speed 100K storage tapes
COLECO ADAM	Yes	No disk	Disk will be available Uses high-speed 256K storage tape (but problems of data loss have occurred because of its design) One tape drive included
APPLE IIe	No	143K	Adequate for storing a series of small-to-medium size files and programs Very long documents (over 50–75 pages) in word processing can't fit on one disk
KAYPRO II	No	200K	Two disk drives included (400K total) Good for word processing and making backup copies of disks easily (using second drive)
IBM PCjr (expanded model)	Yes	360K	One disk drive included Cannot have more than one drive; significant expansion limitation However, one 360K disk holds a large amount of information (150–200 pages)

will need to buy more memory as well; computers usually require more memory to run a disk drive than a cassette, because a bigger set of operating instructions is required and this "sits" in a part of the computer memory reserved for it.

Most computers can use more than one kind of storage. Not all have disks; not all have cartridges; but almost all computers allow you to attach a cassette.

Computer Fact 17: External storage comes via cassette, disk, or cartridge. Almost all computers allow storage on cassettes, but vary in their ability to accept disks and cartridges.

We can compare external storage methods according to the need for special equipment, price, speed, reliability, capacity, and ease of use. There are advantages and trade-offs among the different media.

To use cassette software, you need a cassette player, usually a standard cassette player. For a disk, you need a disk drive. Most personal computers use 5¼-inch drives and disks (with capacity from 80K to 360K and up). Some allow you to use 8-inch drives and their disks, which hold far more information, on the order of 500K or 1,000K (one megabyte, or one million bytes).[4] Some use newer 3-inch disks, which hold as much as a standard 5¼-inch disk. A cartridge usually requires no special hardware at all to access its information; you plug it into the computer itself.[5]

A cassette player is much less expensive than a disk drive. Typically a cassette player costs about $50 while a 5¼-inch disk drive costs $200 to $600. The 3-inch drives are less expensive than the 5¼-inch drives; the 8-inch drives, more expensive.

---

[4] Winchester-type *hard disks* hold even more information—5, 10, 20 megabytes or more. But they are generally not removable, unlike flexible (floppy) diskettes, so you can't substitute one for another and store them on the shelf. They cost $1000–$2000 or more. (For a child with a handicap severe enough to prevent his putting disks into the machine and taking them out, such a device could be very helpful.)

[5] In the future, optical disks, similar to videodiscs, will probably be available for storage and will store billions of bytes of information, as well as audio and video signals, all directly accessible.

Once you have the player or drive, cassette software ranges in price from $10 to $20; disk software, from $20 to several hundred dollars for complex business programs. Cartridges cost $25 and up. For storing your own data, or programs that you write yourself, blank cassettes, which are standard audio cassettes, cost less than disks (some systems use digital cassettes that are a little more expensive), but the prices of both kinds of blank cassettes and of disks are in the $1.50 to $5.00 range. You can't store your own programs on cartridges. Remember, cartridges are ROM memory chips and have information permanently stored on them, so you can't change them. If you use cartridge software where you need to store something, like word-processed text, you use a cassette or disk for storage.

Cartridges are the fastest way to load a program, disks are quite fast, cassettes are generally slow.

A disk drive can find any program on the disk at any time. A cassette player may have to play through several programs on the tape before it comes to the one you want. A new kind of storage device is a cassette player that can quickly fast-forward or rewind to locate information on the tape so you won't have to wait long for the cassette to load. The price is somewhat greater than an ordinary cassette player but less than a disk drive. Coleco's Adam uses this type of storage.

No medium is entirely reliable; things always go wrong, but cartridges are the most reliable. Cassettes are generally reliable, but sometimes you run into problems with the volume setting of the player and have to try many times to load the recorded program. Disks are much more fragile than the other media, easily damaged by dust or bending or a paper clip, but they are quite manageable nonetheless, and children commonly use them.

Cartridges are the easiest to use; you just plug them in. Cassettes and disks are not quite as easy to use. To use cassettes you type a command and turn on the player. Disk software you buy usually loads automatically, but you need to type special commands to load or save your own programs.

For many children, especially where cost or ease of use are critical, cassettes or cartridges are the best choice. However, not all software is available on cartridge or cassette. Where speed of retrieving or storing information is critical, as in word processing, disk storage is preferable. It is also preferable when the task is complex and the program is long. In Chapter 5 we'll describe the kind of storage needed for different activities.

Figure 3–1 showed the basic categories of a computer system—input, output, processing, and storage. *Figure 3–12* shows these same categories, this time with the full range of computer components that fall into each category.

FIGURE 3–12 / **Basic Parts of a Computer System: The Range of Possibilities to Choose From**

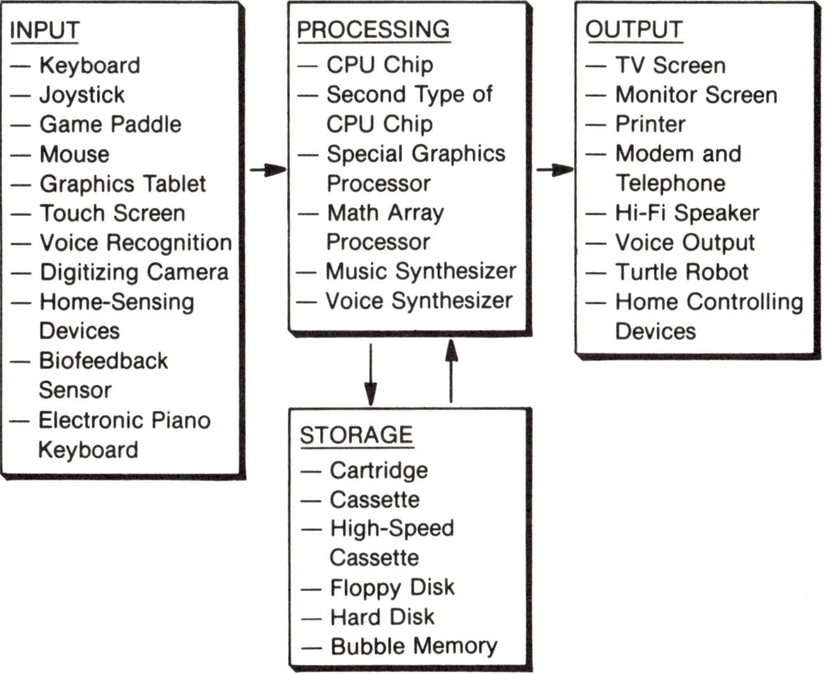

At this point you've covered the basics of computers. The section that follows describes some more technical aspects of computer chips, operating systems, and languages. You may want to skip this section now and return to it later if you find (in Chapter 5) that you need some of this information to select a computer for your child.

HOW THE COMPUTER DOES ITS WORK

The purpose of this section is to help you understand some of the terms that you hear when computers are being described. Generally speaking, you won't need to be very knowledgeable about these terms to buy a computer, but some knowledge will help you in evaluating various products. And it should also help in removing confusion about what kinds of software will work on what computers.

Chips

The work of a microcomputer is done by *chips*. A chip is a tiny silicon wafer containing miniaturized circuitry. There are a number of different kinds of chips in a microcomputer. The microprocessor chip processes the information (it's the Central Processing Unit), the memory chip stores information, and there are often specialized chips to do graphics, voice synthesis, fast arithmetic, or other specialized tasks.

The name of the microprocessor chip is often used to refer to the computer itself. An Apple computer, for example, is a "6502 machine" because its processor is the 6502 chip. Many other computers also use the 6502 chip. (The Atari 600XL and 800XL and the Commodore VIC20 are 6502 machines.) The Radio Shack Model 1, 2, 4, and 12 computers use the Z-80 family of chips. IBM uses the 8088 chip. The Apple Macintosh and Radio Shack Model 16 use the Motorola 68000 chip.

Other terms that you hear when you're buying a computer are "8-bit," "16-bit," and "32-bit machines." A *bit* is the smallest storage unit of a computer. Eight bits make a byte (remember a byte holds a character). On the majority of personal computers, the chip handles one byte or character at a time. On some newer machines, the CPU can handle 16 bits, or two characters, at a time. (Large computers, the kind that cost tens of thousands or even millions of dollars, called *minis* and *mainframes*, are 16-, 32-, or 64-bit machines, but the CPU's are not on a single chip.) Roughly speaking, a 16-bit chip can handle twice as much information at the same time as an 8-bit chip. The 16-bit machine will thus be faster. There is also a relationship between the number of bits a computer can handle and the total size of memory that the computer can easily work with, so that a 16-bit machine can handle a larger memory better than an 8-bit machine. An 8-bit machine is normally limited to handling only 64K bytes of memory unless rather complicated techniques are used, while a 16-bit machine with the right design can handle a million or more bytes, and at the very least can handle 128K, 256K, or 512K, depending on the design.

Operating Systems.

To be able to handle information and transfer it to different parts of the computer and to peripherals like printers and disk drives, the computer needs a set of instructions called an *operating system*. The operating system "knows" how to move things in and out of memory, how to store information on disks and find it again, and how to manage the computer generally. A computer can't "read" a program from another computer's disk when the operating systems are different because the two computers expect to find things stored in different ways on the disk. Generally, computers have different operating systems.

"CP/M," "MS-DOS" (or, on the IBM, "PC-DOS"), "TRSDOS" (for the TRS-80), "UNIX" (available on some larger personal computers), and "VALDOCS" (for the Epson QX-10), are names of operating systems. New versions of operating systems are often given numbers, so Apple's DOS 3.3 is a newer version of the operating system than DOS 3.2. Generally, the newer operating systems can handle programs written with the older system, but not vice versa.

Many different computers can use the CP/M operating system. It requires the 8080 or Z–80 chip. When you use CP/M, you know that any CP/M program will run on your machine. If you have an 8-inch disk drive, you can run any CP/M program on any 8-inch disk. If you have a 5¼-inch drive, you will have to get a CP/M program placed on a disk compatible with your computer. A store or the vendor will do this for you. CP/M programs tend to be for sophisticated applications like word processing and database management.

MS-DOS runs on the 8086 and 8088 family of chips. It is the most popular operating system for 16-bit machines, and runs on IBM and various other personal computers, most of them business-oriented systems. Much software written for the IBM will run on other MS-DOS systems, provided that the software is put into their disk formats and doesn't use special IBM graphics features.

UNIX is a minicomputer operating system from Western Electric/Bell Labs. It is a very flexible and powerful operating system. Versions of UNIX such as XENIX (from Microsoft), which contain some UNIX features, are also available for 16-bit chips such as the 8086 and the 8088 and 32-bit chips such as the Motorola 68000.

Figure 3–13 indicates the types of CPU chip used in some systems and the operating systems associated with them. You probably won't buy a computer just because of its chip, but if your child wants, for example, to use the CP/M operating system for word processing, you should be sure that the computer you buy has a chip that runs CP/M. (*Figure 3–13* contains more technical information than you need, and also contains a number of business-oriented computers, but we feel it may help you organize the diverse world of small computers into simple familiar categories, especially if you are also getting a computer for your own use.)

Languages

A program, which is really instructions to the computer, must be written in a *programming language* that the computer can understand and interpret. A number of different languages are available for personal computers.

Each chip has associated with it a *machine language*, which is the set of commands or individual small steps that the computer chip can follow. The chip also has an *assembly language* that allows the programmer to write abbreviated symbolic instructions that translate directly into machine language for the computer. Assembly language programs are difficult to write and are not something beginners usually get involved with.

Other programming languages, called *high-level languages*,

FIGURE 3–13 / **Types of CPU Chips and Associated Operating Systems**

(Arranged by Increasing Power and Speed of CPU Chip)

Micro-processor Chip (and mfgr.)	Number of Bits	Major Operating Systems	Examples of Computers Using Chip	Comments
6809 FAMILY (MOTOROLA)	8	Varied operating systems	RADIO SHACK COLOR COMPUTER 2	
6502 FAMILY (MOSTEK)	8	Varied operating systems	APPLE IIe ATARI COMMODORE 64	
8080 (INTEL) AND Z–80 (ZILOG) FAMILY	8	CP/M (CP/M-80) TURBO-DOS TRSDOS VALDOCS	COLECO ADAM EPSON QX-10 KAYPRO II RADIO SHACK MODEL 4	Available by plug-in board for APPLE IIe Z–80A is twice as fast as Z–80 Z–80B is three times as fast as Z–80
8088 (INTEL)	16*	MS-DOS CP/M-86 XENIX	DEC RAINBOW 100 IBM PC IBM PCjr	Available by plug-in boards for APPLE IIe and KAYPRO II
8086 FAMILY (INTEL)	16	MS-DOS CP/M-86 XENIX	EAGLE 1600 MINDSET NEC APC WANG PC	Faster versions of the 8086 include the 80186 (used by the Mindset) and the 80286
68000 FAMILY (MOTOROLA)	32**	Varied operating systems including versions of UNIX	APPLE LISA APPLE MACINTOSH RADIO SHACK MODEL 16 SINCLAIR QL	Available by plug-in board for RADIO SHACK Model 12

* 16-bit processor, but only 8-bit data movement (HYBRID 16/8)
** 32-bit processor, but only 16-bit or 8-bit data movement (HYBRID 32/16 or 32/8)

use many English-language commands. These high-level instructions are translated for the chip and turned into machine language before or while the program is being used.

The most common high-level language on personal computers is BASIC. It is a fairly easy language for beginners to learn. BASIC on different computers differs slightly in rules, limitations, and features, but it is usually easy to pick up a new BASIC once you've learned one version of the language. A child who has learned BASIC on a computer at school should find it fairly easy to learn BASIC on a different computer at home, for example. Most BASIC languages allow some graphics commands, and these will differ greatly from computer to computer. Versions of BASIC may also vary to a lesser extent in the use of arrays (tables) and strings (alphabetic characters and symbols).

It is easy to write programs in BASIC, but it is easy to write poorly designed programs too. Languages like Pascal are harder to use but make it easier to write good programs, especially complex programs that run without error and are easy to modify. Many programmers go on from learning BASIC to learning Pascal.

Another good beginner's language, especially for young children, is Logo. Logo is available on a number of personal computers, although it differs slightly from computer to computer. Logo usually has a special graphics language called Turtle Graphics that is easy for young children to use and that allows them to learn some concepts of geometry while they program graphics. Other enhancements of Logo, available on some Logo versions, include *sprites* (invisible carriers of graphics that move across the screen to produce animation), and *list processing* capabilities (a special way to organize information inside the computer by establishing lists that point to other lists).

A COMPUTER SYSTEM FOR A CHILD

An ideal computer system for a child is one that a child can use almost without assistance. The hook-ups between components of the system should be simple, programs should be easy to load, and the operating system should be one that makes it very clear what is to be done at each step. In reality, even with very simple systems, a child needs some help setting up the computer the first time. The systems that are easiest for a child to use are those that are the least powerful. To get the features your child needs, however, you may have to buy a computer system that is more complex and more difficult for your child to use.

Picking a computer system for a child does not simply mean picking a cheap computer. Price should be only one of many factors to take into consideration in buying a computer for a child. Although for many parents an inexpensive computer may be the most logical choice when they don't know how much their child will use the computer, it makes no sense to buy a cheap computer that won't do what your child needs it to do. It makes no sense, for example, to buy an inexpensive computer whose graphics are very difficult to use if your child is artistic and wants to do graphics. By evaluating different systems, you might well find one for the same price, or slightly more, that will have much better graphics.

TRENDS IN COMPUTER HARDWARE

The computer market changes quickly. New products are coming out all the time, and the older products are improved as well. Many people are reluctant to buy a computer now because they assume that next year there will be a better, cheaper product available. Of course, next year, they will still have to contend with the idea of even newer products emerging in the following year. The best solution to the dilemma is to pick out a computer that meets your child's needs today and the needs you project for the future. Recognize that this won't necessarily be the last computer you ever buy the child. As the child's needs change and as computers change, you may well find a compelling reason to change computer systems.

Some parents expect that computer prices will be like calculator prices, constantly descending until the computers that cost a huge sum a few years ago will be available for a few dollars. It is true that the prices of many systems have come down in the last few years, but there are always new computers at higher prices. These higher-priced computers give you more features than the old computers did for the same price. This is the real trend in computers; more features for the same money.

As more features are available, the standards of the industry change also. Where a computer with 4K of memory was common when home computers first came out in 1977, most computers today have far more memory than this available as standard or optional features: 16K, 32K, 64K, and more. This trend will accelerate because the price of memory is plummeting. Similar trends are occurring in graphics, number of bits handled by the CPU (8, 16, 32), number of languages available, and so forth.

At this point, you should have a grasp of some of the basics of computers. Don't be concerned if you can't recall too much detail from this chapter now; you'll probably find that as we refer to these computer features in later chapters, you'll recall the information you need or you can reread this chapter or use the index to review it.

Next, in Chapter 4, we're going to turn to a topic that is much more complex than computers—your child. As complicated as computers may seem, they can't approach the variety and depth of human beings.

Your Child and the Computer

No one knows your child better than you do. But to decide which computer activities fit your child best, you may need to think about your child a little differently. In this chapter we'll help you to develop a profile of your child and to match that profile to computer activities that he will enjoy and that will help him grow.

Keep in mind that you're not trying to play the role of a teacher or psychologist, but simply trying to get a clearer picture of how computers fit into your child's life. You should probably get your child's help in this process, but be careful to keep your discussions fun and friendly. Above all, using computers should be fun for children, and you want to make the whole process of buying and using a computer enjoyable for both of you.

Once you've selected some computer activities based on your knowledge of your child, you'll be ready, in the next chapter, to find a computer system that will let you accomplish these goals.

LOOKING AT CHILDREN AND COMPUTERS

When we talk about your child's interests, we mean almost anything that absorbs his attention. This may be academic areas that are of real interest to your child outside school, special talents, or hobbies. Understanding your child's interests will help you pick computer activities that will fit these interests and that you can be sure your child will enjoy.

You should also look at academic needs. In what areas does your child need extra help; in what areas are special strengths evident? You'll be able to pick out some educational computer applications that also fit your child's needs.

The area of careers is a sensitive one. Even though many people are saying that computer knowledge is absolutely essential to job success in the future, keep in mind that this is an extreme view. Don't feel that if you don't buy a computer, your child will not be successful in a career. Even if computer exposure is necessary, there are many other ways to gain this experience when it is needed. Also, remember that the nature of the computer knowledge that will be needed for future careers may change as new computer technology and software tools evolve.

The way you look at careers will depend on your child's age. Although today's children may be thinking about which careers they will pursue much earlier than their parents did, you certainly don't want to encourage a child of ten to make a career choice. For a high-school senior, however, it is quite reasonable to buy a computer with the idea that it will help in his studies for a certain career.

You'll also be looking at some personality factors in this chapter. Each child has specific learning styles that should be taken into account when selecting hardware and software. Once again, you'll be looking at ways to tailor a computer activity to your child's own special style.

Finally, we will examine the special needs some children have because of learning or physical disabilities, and how these affect computer use for those children.

Let's see how this kind of approach works for some children with different kinds of profiles.

Sarah is a six-year-old with a talent for drawing. She is more interested in the results of her drawing efforts than in the process itself and likes to hang her pictures up in her room. Sarah might enjoy working with computer graphics. Because of her age and her interest in results, she needs a graphics package that is simple to use and produces quick results. One of the computer systems with a software package that uses a joystick (pots of paint show on the screen and you dip a "brush" into one by moving it with the joystick) might be a good choice for her. Her parents might also consider getting an inexpensive color printer so that she can print her drawings on paper.

Beth is a high-school student with a strong interest in math who thinks that computers might be a career for her. She might benefit greatly from using a computer to learn programming. Beth needs a real "programmer's" computer, with a number of different available languages.

Nathaniel has been diagnosed by his school as having a learning disability. He has difficulty handling detail and responding quickly. He likes to play games and wants to be able to play video games "like the other kids," but because he can't deal with the requirement for rapid response, traditional video games are frustrating for him. Nathaniel can handle some educational video games that don't require instant response and other games that don't have too much detail on the screen at once. Games where he can select a level of difficulty are also a good choice.

David is a fourth-grader having trouble with reading in school. He also likes games. For David, computer reading games are a possible activity, as are other games where the reading level for the game instructions is low and where he will want to master the reading so he can play the game. In the preceding example of Nathaniel, the computer will allow a child to participate in an activity that is closed to him otherwise, but won't necessarily help with his learning problem. In David's case the computer can help overcome the problem.

How Does Your Child Feel about Computers?

What point is your child at now? Has your child developed a sense of what he would like to do with a computer? It's important that a child be able to picture the kinds of activities that can be done with the computer before you buy it. When you got married did you receive a wedding gift you couldn't identify much less imagine how to use? You don't want to put your child into that position with a computer. You want your child to develop, along with you, a sense of what this purchase will mean.

One parent has offered her children a choice: They receive several dollars a week apiece to spend on video arcade games or to save. The children have decided to save the money to buy a computer because they realize they will get to play far more video games for the same money with their own computer. Their mother is also showing them that the computer has other interesting uses, such as teaching them to type. They have a real sense of what the computer will mean to them.

Your child might be one who has researched the computer area and has picked out a computer for the use he has in mind. If this is so, you should compliment your child on the research done and find out just why he picked that particular computer and activity. Your child may be telling you something about his interests that you didn't know. You should then check the decision your child has made, following the strategy and the charts in this book to be sure that the computer he selected is the right one. You may have to extend his thinking a bit to take into account other computer activities that come to mind as you consider his interests and needs. Your child may be right on target, or you may find that there is a better choice. Work with your child to make and explain these decisions. Don't just take over the process when your child has shown this kind of motivation.

Your child may be one who has not done any real research but has an interest in a particular computer activity that he has heard about. You will probably want to broaden the child's awareness of computer activities by working through this chapter together. Then, in the next chapter, you'll need to select computer hardware for these activities.

Some children simply think a computer would be fun, will help them get a job, and so forth, but can't give any examples of what they would like to do with the computer. This kind of child differs from the previously mentioned ones in that he has no particular activity in mind. (Most children are aware of the game playing ability of the computer, so a vague wish to play games doesn't count here.) This child needs to become a little more knowledgeable about computers. Showing him computers and software in a computer store and letting him try out software and hardware will help him to see what computers are like, and you can see how he responds to the kind of activities you think are appropriate.

Some children seem either to be turned off by computers or simply unaware of them. Very young children, in particular, will fall into this category. Again, as in the previous case, you should work with this child a bit before you present him with a computer. If he has a fear of math that he is transferring to computers, you have to show him that computers are not mathematical tools but versatile, general tools that apply as much to art and language and other interests as they do to math. If the child is "antitechnology," you can try to show how the computer will help him do things he really cares about.

Certainly you shouldn't buy a computer for a child who really doesn't want one, nor should you force him to do a computer activity that he doesn't want to do. Keep in mind, though, that your child may change his opinion of either computers or a computer activity. One ten-year-old girl didn't want to use a word processor because none of the other children in school did their papers that way, and she didn't want to be different. She was encouraged to try it just once, found that it was much easier to do her work, and decided to become a nonconformist in this area.

Bear in mind that especially for a child without a clear sense of wanting a computer, the first computer experience should be pleasant and successful and should connect to other interests the child has. If you want to have your child do math drill on the computer because he doesn't do well at math, it might be better to start out with an activity like games or storywriting, where he will feel more comfortable and successful, before going on to math drill.

YOUR CHILD'S INTERESTS

Look first at your child's current interests. Many of these interests will lead you directly to some related computer activities. As a result, your child will be motivated to use the computer and will feel comfortable working on familiar activities. The computer may help your child do better in his area of interest and may lead him to new interests that the computer can also help with. For example, a child who likes music can play music on the computer and improve his skills. He may then use the computer to try composing as well.

Certainly you are aware of many of your child's interests, but it might be helpful to make a list of them to have in front of you. Then you might discuss the list with your child. (If you're not sure what all your child's interests are, start with a list of things he's done and enjoyed in the last year.) Be sure to include in your list those interests that your child shows a lot of enthusiasm for and spends time on, not just the areas in which he shows a lot of talent. For example, your young child may spend a great deal of time drawing animals, but you can't tell his ducks from his cats. This child is obviously finding some reward in drawing, and would probably enjoy using computer graphics. You might find that computer graphics let him really enjoy the aspect of drawing he finds interesting—perhaps it's playing with colors that he really likes.

Below is a list of the interests we cover in this chapter. In the following sections, we'll discuss computer activities to go with each interest. Compare your list of your child's interests to this list and check off the ones we cover. You'll want to read these sections of course, but skim the other sections as well. You may find an activity there that appeals to you or your child.

AREAS OF INTEREST

Creative Interests
     Drawing
     Music
     Writing
     Photography
     Videotape
Reading
Collecting
Science/Math
     Ecology/nature study
     Science
     Math

Physical Activities
      Dance
      Sports
Cars
Space (Star Wars, etc.)
Models
Family history and family trees
Puzzles and games
Amateur radio
Politics and current events
Mechanical and electronic interests (fixing and building
    things)
Imaginative play
Programming
Robotics (ties in with programming, electronics, computer
    science)

Organizing Your Analysis

When you select computer hardware and software, it's important that you have very clearly in your mind what activities your child will engage in with computers and how these activities will meet your child's needs. One way to focus your search is to make a chart like the one following. The chart will show you at a glance what your child's interests and needs are, what computer activities will meet those needs, what special features to look for, and what kinds of hardware and software you'll need to buy to accomplish your goals.

	Topic	Computer Activity	Special Features	Hardware/ Software
INTERESTS				
ACADEMIC				
CAREER				

For now, we will look at the first row in the left column, "Interests." Later in the chapter, you'll be able to fill in the "Academic" and "Career" rows. The first heading in the top row, "Topic," refers to topics of interest to your child. For example, drawing is an interest for Sarah, the young girl we discussed at the beginning of the chapter. "Activity" refers to the kind of computer activity that fits the topic; for Sarah, it's computer graphics. "Special Features" refers to the special characteristics that an activity must have to fit your child; for Sarah, the computer graphics software package must be simple and printed copies of her pictures would be nice. "Hardware/ Software" needs will be filled in later. Here's what the interests section of the chart would look like for Sarah:

	Topic	Computer Activity	Special Features	Hardware/ Software
INTERESTS	Drawing	Computer graphics	Easy to use; printed copy	(To come in Chapter 5)
ACADEMIC				
CAREER				

You're now ready to make a chart and fill in the topics of interest to your child. Then read on to find the computer activities that fit these interests.

Programming as a Component of Other Activities

Although we will deal later with programming as a computer activity by itself, many of the activities mentioned in this chapter require some programming. For example, we'll discuss a child who wants to create music on the computer, by using the BASIC language to command the computer to produce sounds, and a child who wants to use the computer to help with calculations for science homework. These children and others will need to do computer programming to accomplish their goals. The complexity of the programming needed for different activities varies, and we'll indicate what level is needed.

Children's ability to handle programming, either as a separate activity or as part of another activity, varies with the individual child and with age. Generally speaking, preschool and kindergarten children can't handle programming at all. They can't read or write English well, so they certainly can't construct programs in a computer language. They also lack the logic skills needed for programming. However, they might be able to manage the simple "programming" needed for the Bigtrack toy (see below, under Models) or for the simplest Logo programming.

From first grade up, programming abilities improve. Children from first to third grade can do simple programming, in the Logo language and in BASIC. They can do some simple graphics and music programming. From fourth grade through junior high, a child's ability to learn and handle programming rapidly increases. By junior high, children can learn and do sophisticated programming, including complex graphics. By high school, children are capable of doing almost any programming that an adult can do. Their level of programming skill will depend on the instruction they get, the amount of experience they've had, and their individual aptitude.

This is true for children of any age. Programming is not a natural skill; children need instruction (whether from a computer manual, computer teaching program, book, magazine, or computer course) in order to do any programming, and they need practice in programming. If you and your child decide that he wants to do an activity that involves programming, first be sure that he is old enough to handle the level of programming involved. Then be sure he has the support needed to master the skill.

Creative Interests

For a child interested in art, computer graphics are a natural match, and there is virtually no limit to what can be done with computer graphics by a creative person with the right equipment. Your child might do graphics with a graphics tablet or with a piece of software that lets him draw on the screen, such as Delta Drawing Learning Program by Spinnaker. By stringing together a series of predrawn graphics, the child can produce a kind of "slide show" of images on the screen. Such a show could accompany a friend playing a musical instrument or synthesizer.

The child might want to use graphics packages that let him

animate his drawings. Facemaker by Spinnaker does this at a simple level; Graphics Magician by Penguin does it at a more sophisticated level. Software for the Mindset computer does it at both levels. Animation usually requires some programming knowledge.

The child might want to program graphics, with Logo and Turtle Graphics, with the Pilot language, or with an all-purpose programming language like BASIC. Programming graphics takes much longer than drawing on the screen, but it offers a chance to learn programming through an activity that is of interest to the child. Graphics programming can be done at a very simple level; it's actually a good way to learn programming. Sophisticated graphics and animation require complex programs.

A child interested in music can perform or compose music on a computer with music capabilities. A synthesizer or a software package like Music Construction Set from Electronic Arts that allows easy composing and saving of pieces will help. The child can do simple programming of music directly through a language like BASIC, but probably will find it very tedious and not a very good learning tool. Other software teaches note recognition and music theory.

If your child is interested in writing, the computer's word-processing abilities can be very helpful. Most, if not all, of today's computers can be used as word processors with special software, a printer, and, usually, disk drives. A program that checks spelling would be useful too. A younger child who likes to write might enjoy the "story-making" software that helps a child to create a story or enjoy an adventure-type game where he can add parts to the adventure. Some software allows the child to create different characters and settings and use them in a number of adventure games.

Writing plays is a special application of the word processor. Using the computer makes it easier to write plays for friends to perform. Changes in the script can be made easily. With a printer, the child can print a copy of the play for each participant.

A child who would like to produce a neighborhood newspaper can use the word processor as well. It will be particularly helpful for items repeated in each issue, like ads, credits, headings, or for sections which change little from issue to issue. A word processor allows you to pick up sections from one issue, make minor changes, and include them in the next. (Hardware and software that lets you easily insert graphics material into a text document could be very helpful in producing a newspaper or newsletter. The Macintosh is a good example of a computer with this ability.)

You may find that a child with a word processor writes more letters to grandparents and friends, printing and mailing some letters and sending others by electronic mail, using a modem to communicate with another computer.

New software developed on large computers and now becoming available on microcomputers can help tremendously in writing. These packages do some analysis of the writing entered into a word processor. Typically they point out overused adjectives, questionable usage, overuse of passive verbs, and some grammatical errors. Some also report the length of sentences, difficulty level of the passage, clarity of organization, and a number of other useful things. As these become more sophisticated, analysis of writing will become a very valuable computer activity for the child who likes to write, or wants to improve his writing. Such tools as Writer's Workbench (from Bell Labs/Western Electric), Punctuation & Style, and Grammatik are already finding their way into colleges. (Writer's Workbench is very expensive and runs only on UNIX-based computers, but is very comprehensive. Punctuation & Style and Grammatik are simpler programs with many of the same features. They are moderately priced and run on the IBM PC and other computers.)

Photography is an interest that leads to a new computer activity—storing and altering pictures on a computer screen. When the Sony Mavica camera becomes available (its design was announced several years ago but the product has been delayed in reaching the market), you will be able to take a picture and show it on the screen, store it on disk, and print it out in color on a color printer. Using other techniques, it is also possible to modify and superimpose images, and send pictures over phone lines to another computer.

Videotaping and viewing is becoming a new hobby for adults and children alike. In the future, home-video and home-computer technology will increasingly converge. Some computer manufacturers, notably Sharp, are working on home-entertainment packages that permit you to first buy a computer and then add on video equipment that can be connected to it and vice versa. For a child with a serious interest in videotape, transferring the video screen output of a computer animation or simulation onto videotape, editing it together with other video films, and showing them on the TV screen could be a very exciting activity.

The Sharp X–1 system (currently sold only in Japan) even allows you to extract a freeze-frame from videotape, superimpose a computer-generated graphic onto it, display the combined image on a monitor, and create a hard copy transparency. A child whose family has a videotape system might also want to use the filing and data retrieval features of a computer to keep track of a collection of tapes.

Reading

A child who likes to read will probably enjoy the various adventure games available for personal computers. You're probably familiar with the general format of an adventure game. Typically it presents text on the screen describing a situation, and allows you to describe the action you want to take, like "Walk north." As you progress through the adventure, trying to find a treasure or slay a dragon or whatever, you constantly encounter new situations. You can play an adventure game many times, even after you solve the puzzle, because there are so many different paths through the adventure. Some of the newer games present a good deal of the story in graphics. A child who likes to read might enjoy being able to interact with the story. Adventure game stories include science fiction, mysteries, fairy tales, dungeon-and-dragon type stories, etc. One series of adventure games, from Rhiannon, is designed especially for girls and includes, for example, a story about a pioneer girl on her own on the prairie. The Snooper Troops programs from Spinnaker allow children to solve a mystery.

Reading is a good example of a case where a child's interest can lead to enjoyment of the computer and also to developing other skills. A child who enjoys playing adventure games because of the story will also have to develop some reasoning and interpreting skills and a good strategy, in order to play the game successfully.

Children who like reading might also like vocabulary games and linguistic games, and might want to create their own stories with a story-maker program or a word processor.

Speed-reading software is also available, such as the package marketed by Atari.

Collecting

Children who like to collect things are likely to be interested in sorting and categorizing their collections. One child who collects stamps, for example, spends a good deal of time making lists of his stamps by country. A simple-to-use database system would enable a collecting child like this to update records, sort through for a particular item, print out alphabetized or sorted lists on a printer, and count items of different types. In the process, the child would learn how to create and manipulate a database, which is a very valuable computer skill in itself. (The Sinclair QL is a relatively low-cost computer that includes a database program without extra charge.)

A collecting child might also want to use the computer to learn more about the items he collects. A rock collector might want to learn some earth science, a shell collector might want to learn about oceanography, etc. Check for available software in the areas your child might be interested in.

With a modem and access to a local computer bulletin board, the child might also stay in touch with other people in the area who share his interests.

Science/Math

A child interested in science has the opportunity to use the computer in science simulations in a wide variety of areas. Simulations allow the child to do experiments that are impossible to do at home or even at school, without special equipment, and to watch a scientific process, like atomic activity, that would be impossible even with equipment. The child can manipulate the elements of the process to gain insight.

A television series that combines computers with science shows the computer in use on an expedition to study whales and allows children in the classroom to duplicate some of the experiments. Your child, too, might want to use the computer to try something he has read about or seen in a science film. Or he can use the computer to do calculations to assist in his schoolwork, to prepare for a science fair, etc. Doing these activities usually requires some knowledge of programming. Doing calculations is a simple programming task. Simulating a science task can require complex programming, but a child can often find a way to imitate something he's seen without straining his programming ability.

An interest in math might lead to programming (see the section on programming below) and then to doing probability experiments on the computer, investigating symmetries with graphics, and using math educational software on advanced topics to move ahead in math. For the lower grades, this could mean exploring fractions; for the higher grades, exploring the nature of calculus, or special topics such as Buckminster Fuller's geometry concepts. The important contribution of the computer is in aiding the student in the development of insight and intuition. This is accomplished through interaction with repeated concrete examples of mathematical objects and relationships in graphic or numeric form. A child can examine, for example, the behavior of various mathematical functions or the properties of geometric figures. This is especially valuable in the study of three-dimensional figures, because they can be rotated on the screen to enable the student to see them from different perspectives.

Physical Activities

For a child who is interested in playing active games, dancing, doing gymnastics, and playing sports, you may need to find special ways to relate your child's interests to the computer. As a start, you might find that video games, where there is a lot of action on the screen and where it is necessary to manipulate a joystick, are interesting to your child. If he is good at sports, your child may also be very good at this kind of coordination. Computer baseball, football, or basketball games where the player has to work on a game strategy may also be of interest.

Several children who are baseball fans have used the computer to keep track of statistics on their favorite teams. Your child could do this, either by writing fairly simple programs himself or using a simple database filing system.

A computer can be a great aid to athletes and dancers. Using larger computers, sports medicine programs developed at universities analyze athletic movement and also sometimes use biofeedback techniques. Other programs sketch dancers in motion. Personal computer software for this kind of activity is rare at the moment, although this is changing. For example, the DOM (Dance on Microcomputer) system, written for the Apple by Eddie Dombrower, lets a choreographer create a sequence of body movements to be carried out by a dancing figure on the screen. These can be stored on disk, played back, and later modified. Also, biofeedback games exist (such as those from Thought Technology in Montreal) that help you learn how to reduce stress. Biofeedback games have been written by Dr. John Gianutsas of the NYU Institute of Rehabilitation Medicine in New York to help handicapped children improve motor coordination.

Ideally, the computer would allow a young person to explore and analyze movement on the computer screen to determine the most effective way to perform different activities. It would also allow the child to choreograph a dance and see groups of small figures moving in the patterns of the dance. Until more dance and movement software is widely available, you may have to find other areas of interest to capitalize on. Perhaps your child likes art as well as dance, and you can promote computer graphics and the imaginative use of color, sound, and rhythm.

There is also a way to program relatively simple movements of figures and shapes around the screen by using something called *sprites*. These are invisible points to which shapes can be attached and whose motion on the screen can be programmed. One system allows sixteen different sprites to move about, each carrying a colored ball or square or some other figure. The sprites feature is available in some versions of the Logo language and on some computers as a feature of BASIC as well, and is usually easy to use.

In addition, for fitness-minded children there are nutrition programs that analyze calorie intake and suggest ways to achieve a balanced diet.

Cars, Space Toys, and Models

A young child interested in cars might like to play with the Bigtrack toy, which is a small car controlled by a hand-held computer. The computer has to be programmed to move the car forward or back, to turn it, and so forth. From controlling only the motion of the car, the child might graduate to a real computer system with turtle graphics that are programmed in a similar way. A young person might also respond well to the many educational software programs with a car or racetrack motif. You can accomplish the goal of getting your child to practice math problems, for example, while he enjoys the race fantasy.

For children interested in space toys, *Star Wars*, and so on, adventure games in a space setting, space video games, and *Star Wars* games might be of interest. A child might also want to pretend that the computer is on board a spaceship and program it to control the make-believe craft. This requires that the child have a moderate skill level at programming. Or a child might use a computer game where he is the captain of a spaceship and must make decisions about its operation.

Children interested in model trains might enjoy using the computer to control the movement of trains. This would require some fairly sophisticated programming knowledge and some knowledge of special hardware, but could be very interesting to an older child.

Family History and Family Trees

Children can also use computer graphics (such as drawing tools) to design a series of sketches for models they will later build from real materials. The same approach can be applied to fashion design. Using the computer makes it easier to alter, vary, and experiment with the design.

A child interested in the history of his family might undertake a number of tasks on the computer, all within the framework of a family-history project. The child might use a genealogy program to represent the family tree on the screen and then redraw the tree each time he adds new information about the family. He might also use a filing program to store and organize facts about the social, economic, and cultural settings of various family members and generations, in this country and abroad. Remote databases could be queried, via a modem, to search for historical information or immigration records. (In 1986, as a part of the hundredth anniversary celebration of the Statue of Liberty, a computer system will allow visitors to Ellis Island to look up the immigration records of anyone who entered the United States through Ellis Island. Perhaps this information will also be made available to personal computer users across the country.)

Puzzles and Games

A large number of games available for computers are not simply action video games. They include Rubik's Cube games, backgammon, chess, word games, crossword puzzles, and bridge. Most of these allow the option of playing against the computer or another person, so a child who can't find someone to play chess with can still practice his game. With a modem and a friend with a similar setup, a child can play chess with someone down the block or across the country.

In the future, games will be even more elaborate. Some may incorporate real-world information such as current baseball team rankings and player averages (from an information service) to make the games more exciting and motivating.

A child interested in game playing might also want to learn programming, so as to program games. Word games are fairly easy to program, but video games require moderate to highly sophisticated programming ability, depending on their graphics complexity. A game like Pinball Construction Set allows you to create your own pinball game and play it, without knowing how to program. The future promises more game-writing capabilities that make use of special techniques such as three-dimensional effects or special accessories such as interactive videodisc.

Amateur Radio

There has been a resurgence of interest in amateur or ham radio in recent years. With a computer, a ham radio operator can practice Morse code (with special software packages). Special interfaces for some computers allow you to type characters on the computer and have them translated by the computer into Morse code and sent out over the ham radio, or to pick up Morse code transmissions, translate them into letters and numbers, and print them out on screen or printer. A ham radio operator should investigate such options through a ham radio interest group in the community. Accessories also exist that allow deaf-blind operators to read Morse code via a small vibrating surface. (Write to Dan Zuckerman, Human Interface Lab, Rensselaer Polytechnic Institute, Troy, NY 12181.)

Politics and Current Events

Computerized news services such as the Dow Jones News Service or the many news services and newspapers available through CompuServe are a lot of fun for someone interested in current events. Your child types a topic he is interested in and waits for the computer to find a story on this topic in its files. Then he has the option of viewing the story on the screen if the title interests him. To use the services, your child would need a modem and a subscription to one or more computer networks. There may be a small one-time connect fee, and then you pay by the minute for use, usually with a credit-card billing.

Mechanical and Electronic Interests

A child can actually build his own computer with kits like those produced by Heathkit if his interests lie in electronics. On a simpler level, a young person can build special peripherals that will be controlled by the computer, perhaps an interface to a printer or something as simple as a bell. There are many computer magazine articles on the hardware side of computers, some of which suggest modifications that a child interested in electronics might like to do. Most of these activities require some real knowledge of electronics, and your child might need to take a training course or put together some simple electronic kits to first learn the basics.

Imaginative Play

Earlier we discussed a case where a child might want to use the computer to pretend to run a spaceship. Children naturally want to do the things adults do; playing house, playing grocery store, and the like, are imitations of and preparation for adult behavior. Children using computers will sometimes also want to pretend that they are doing something adult with the computer. The computer, in this case, can be just another one of the child's toys and can fit into a normal play routine.

To engage in imaginative play with the computer, a child might need to learn some simple programming so that he can produce the kind of screen displays he wants for his game. Or he might use a simple piece of business software to pretend to run a store, a database system to pretend to run a library, an air-traffic controller simulation game to pretend to be in charge of an airport, etc.

Programming

Although we've dealt with programming as an activity that might be appropriate for helping to carry out various other activities, it deserves some consideration as an interest in and of itself. Many children are interested in developing or improving programming skills. A child who has learned computer programming at school or at computer camp may have a particularly strong interest in programming. Such a child might well enjoy a computer where he can do programming in more than one language. The choice of computer language can be a difficult one, involving tradeoffs, so the availability of several languages is probably helpful.

Even children who have not learned any programming may express an interest in programming their own games. In fact, programming games is probably the strongest programming interest among children. Keep in mind that the task of programming a computer game can be one of the most difficult a child can take on, involving graphics, speed of execution and a complex logic. The tasks the child wishes to accomplish may be beyond his powers. Even when you buy a child a computer for programming, you should plan to supply software like programming aids (these are shortcuts such as special editors or "debugging" tools), graphics packages, books, computer magazines, and computer classes to help your child. A child interested in programming might want to join a users' group, made up either of adults or children, in the area. This can be a marvelous outlet for a socially shy child as well.

Robotics

Another area that might turn out to be interesting to your child is robotics. Robots are still rather expensive, but they might be worth the investment to you. A child with a strong interest in computers, electronics, or artificial intelligence could learn a great deal from programming a robot.

A number of different robots are available for use with a personal computer. The Tasman Turtle is a small robot that acts like the "turtle" you see on the screen in turtle graphics. Its moves are directed by Logo, and it can move around the floor or table as long as it doesn't get too far from the computer because it's attached by a cable. It can hold a pen and draw with it as it moves, and it can even speak with a speech synthesizer.

Some robots, like the Androbot, are controlled by a joystick and computer, communicating with the robot via radio signals. The robot can move around the room as directed by the computer, make sounds, flash lights, and so on. It should be possible to program the robot, via the computer and simple computer programming, to do more elaborate actions as well. Some robots have heat sensors and ultrasound and can move around a room sensing objects in their path. Some can simulate the arm movements of a human.

Other Interests

We haven't covered all the possible interests a child might have or all the computer activities that match each interest, but by now you should have a number of activities on your chart. Add others that occur to you. And remember that your child may well express a desire to do some computer activity that doesn't fit any interest that you know about now. When that happens, add those activities to the chart as well.

ACADEMICS

Ways of Learning

Most parents are aware that computers can help their child to do better in school subjects. To use a computer for work in academic areas, your child will generally need to use educational software. You will have to become more knowledgeable about this type of software.

To appreciate educational software, it may be helpful to think of learning as divided into three categories—learning by practicing, learning from presentation, and learning by observing a process and interacting with it.

Some things are best learned by *practicing* them again and again. Multiplication tables, spelling, art techniques, and music performance fall into this category. Although you need some instruction to get you going, most learning takes place during exercise and repetition of the activity.

Some ideas and concepts are learned from *presentation*. Grammar, basic math, and science concepts fall into this category. You may need to practice later, but the presentation of the concepts is most important.

Observing and interacting is useful when you need to understand a relationship between facts, as in understanding how temperature and pressure affect the volume of a gas. The words *experimenting* and *discovering* are also used to describe this process.

Types of Software

The chart on page 98 shows the categories that educational software is generally divided into. You can see from the chart that different types of software are best suited to different types of learning.

Determining Skills to Work On

You probably know what areas your child has difficulty with in school, but to make effective use of computer software, you should be very specific about just what skills you want the software to cover. The more specific the skills you can write on the chart under "Topics," the more likely it is that you will pick out helpful software for your child.

Suppose that a seventh grader has had difficulty with written assignments for years. The problems the child has are in a variety of skill areas including spelling, punctuation, organization of ideas, and vocabulary. In each skill he is at a different

	Definition	Skills	Software Examples
Drill & Practice	A series of problems or questions are presented for the student to answer. Sometimes done in "game" format where the student's points are determined by whether the answer is correct. Doesn't teach concepts. Stresses ability to recall facts, perform calculations, or do simple problem solving.	Learning by practicing	Arithmetic computation drills. Foreign language drill. SAT prep.
Tutorial	Presents information, asks questions, usually "branches" to new information if child is correct and to a review if not. Teaches concepts and basic facts.	Learning from presentation	Grammar lessons. Explanation of how to do math problems.
Simulation	Portrays a process or real-life situation, allowing the student to control some aspects and see the results. Teaches relationships, cause and effect, and analytical skills.	Learning by observing and interacting	Simulate the running of a nuclear plant. Science experiments. History simulation.
Tools	Software not designed to teach but which helps the student carry out a process that is educational in itself. Helps teach both method and content skills.	Learning by observing and interacting	BASIC language. Word processor. Program that does statistical calculations.

level of achievement according to his teachers. So the list of topics for this child would include such items as fifth-grade spelling, basic punctuation, junior-high vocabulary, and general logic and organization skills.

When looking at any academic subject as a possible need for your child, ask yourself these kinds of questions. Is the child just beginning to fall behind in his work? Perhaps the problem is that fundamental skills weren't mastered before and therefore new topics can't be learned. This is the situation with a child who has done all right in math until the fourth grade and then finds he can't handle the multiplication problems in his math book. The difficulty for this child is that he never really learned the multiplication tables well enough to use them in more complex problems. This child needs help in the multiplication tables.

Another child might have learned earlier skills but might be confused by new concepts or requirements. A child who did well in phonics in earlier grades might not be able to handle reading comprehension skills later on. This child would be wasting time reviewing phonics on the computer, but needs software to help in reading comprehension.

In addition to subjects where your child has problems, think about areas where he does very well in school and where you feel he could benefit from some enrichment. These areas might include those in which the child has a strong interest or where the connection to a career choice is clear. Any child studying a new, unfamiliar subject might well benefit from extra work on the computer, to build up insight or skill. Also consider special topics in which the school is unable to provide instruction but for which an introductory experience could help round out or broaden other work the child has done and found interesting. For example, if the child has studied French and Spanish, then an exposure to Italian might prove valuable during a summer vacation.

You may want to talk to teachers or resource people at school. If you're trying to help your child with a problem area, you may well want to coordinate your efforts at home with the school's efforts.

Once you've filled in the "Topic" section of the academic row on your chart, make some notes on your chart about the kind of software that will help meet your child's needs in each specific skill. Our example child, Sarah, who likes to draw, is having trouble remembering to carry in addition. She needs to practice the skill. For Sarah, the chart now looks like this:

	Topic	Computer Activity	Special Features	Hardware/ Software
INTERESTS	Drawing	Computer graphics	Easy to use; printed copy	(To come in Chapter 5)
ACADEMIC	Addition with carrying	Drill & practice	Fun to do	
CAREER				

Computers and College

A college-bound student has some special requirements from a computer. All students can use word processing for writing papers. A student who will be doing a lot of research (a history major, for example) could use database software. A student interested in science, math, or engineering can use a package like TK! Solver that does calculations with formulas and equations. The "TK" stands for "toolkit," and there are modules sold as tools for different occupational areas. A business student might use the VisiCalc package to model business finances and see the results of different decisions.

A student planning to take programming courses in college, whether as part of a major in computer science or not, can use a personal computer for programming. This student might also want to hook up his computer through a modem to the college central computer to work on programs for his computer classes. In effect, he'd use his computer as a "terminal" for that larger computer.

Some Special Skill Areas

There are some skills that might not appear on your list but where the computer could be of great help to your child.

Quite a number of logic games are available for children, including Rocky's Boots from The Learning Company and The Factory from Sunburst. The computer can be very good at helping a child learn logical thinking by allowing him to try out several solutions to a problem to see which one works best.

There are a number of preschool programs available. These can be useful in aiding development of some crucial early learning skills, such as sequencing, color matching, alphabet matching, and simple counting activities.

The computer can be of value in preparing for the SAT college entrance exam. Many of the SAT preparation packages on the market stress practice in taking the test. Educational Testing Service research tends to show that practice does not help that much, but this is an area of controversy. Some of the packages stress test-taking skills or question analysis skills, and these should be helpful.

Learning programming on the computer can also be a great aid in learning other skills such as math and reading. A child won't learn math or reading from programming, but will be motivated to improve these skills in other ways. A child who wants to solve a programming problem will be forced to read manuals to find the answer. A child who has to instruct the computer to do some calculations as part of a game will have to understand some basic math concepts to do that.

CAREERS

In the Career section of the chart, you should put down a number of possible careers that your child might be interested in. (Assuming your child is old enough to make this reasonable to do.) Career interests tend to overlap general interests and academic interests, so there will be some overlap on your chart.

In thinking about how a computer can help your child make a career choice or succeed in a career, consider how the computer might help in learning a relevant subject area. A student considering a career as a doctor might want to do some biology and physiology simulations on the computer, for example. Think also about how computers are used as tools in the field your child has in mind and consider exposing your child to these uses of the computer. One twelve-year-old boy who wants to become a CPA experiments with VisiCalc to learn something about how finance works. A child who wants to be a journalist might learn word processing to see what it is like to write stories on the computer. Using computer software or accessing a computer database can help your child tap into the culture of the career he is interested in.

Also, specialized educational software that is developed at the college level to serve as a campus-wide resource might be made accessible to advanced high-school students by special arrangement as part of a career exploration. (Dr. Terry Mitiken of the University of Texas at San Antonio has written a beautiful series of self-paced introductory software on neuroscience for students in the health sciences. This software, which is filled with rich color graphics, runs on the Apple and can be loaned out to any college student on campus.)

Knowledge of computers can also be helpful to your child in getting a summer job in a field of interest or just to earn money for college. Everyone has heard of the children who make thousands or tens of thousands of dollars by selling their game software, but even if your child doesn't make it into this class, he may still be able to get a summer job as a data entry clerk, working in a computer store, or in a word processing pool because of his experience with a computer.

PERSONALITY AND LEARNING STYLES

At this point you have a good idea of your child's interests and academic and career needs. If you've made a chart, in the second column you have a corresponding list of the computer activities that match these needs. Under "Special Features" you may have some notes on things to look for. Now we'll add to the "Special Features" section by looking at your child's personality and learning style to see how these will affect the type of computer activities that are right for him.

A Caveat

Our advice about tailoring computer activities to fit your child's personality draws on common sense, our experiences, and advice from experts. But this is still a new field where trial and error is the operating principle. No one knows your child as well as you, so don't neglect your experience if it conflicts with our advice.

What It's Like to Use a Computer

Unfortunately, computers and software today are not always simple to use. They aren't always "friendly" to the user. In fact, sometimes they seem designed to confuse you. Even when the computer and software are well designed and easy to use, it's necessary to have a certain set of skills to use the computer effectively.

A child using a computer typically has to read directions in a manual to set up the computer. Then he has to read directions that come with the software (often called *documentation*) to see how to get the software running on the computer. He has to read and follow directions on the screen, perhaps make a decision on what level of game to play, and understand the feedback the computer gives. A good deal of patience is needed for all of this, plus the ability to read and follow directions.

When Lisa uses the database system for her rock collection, she has to structure and plan her use of the software ahead of time in order to use it effectively. She also has to tolerate occasional problems when, for one reason or another, she loses some work done on the computer and has to reconstruct it. Computer use often requires an organized, systematic approach as well as tolerance of frustration.

A child doing programming has to plan the program, invent new ways of doing things, find errors, and struggle with the program until it works. It can take a tremendous amount of patience to follow through this process to the end.

A child using graphics on the computer has to learn a new medium, including limitations and special rules, read directions for using some occasionally complicated commands, and persist in figuring out how to get the effects he wants. The child has to have the creativity to deal with the new environment and be willing to experiment to find techniques that work.

You can see that computer use can call for such characteristics as persistence, creativity, tolerance of frustration, ability to read and understand information, etc. But some computer activities and some computers and software packages make greater demands than others. It is possible to choose computer activities, individual computers, and software to fit your child's personality.

Task Commitment

The first personality trait we'll look at is what we might call "task commitment." It refers to the persistence and drive to complete a task despite setbacks. This trait has been tied to success in learning to program, and it is helpful in many other computer activities as well.

To see to what degree this is part of your child's make-up, ask yourself what will usually happen when your child starts a project (a model, Lego town, picture, story, sewing, reading, etc.) that will take some time to complete. Will he stick to the task, returning to it as necessary, asking for help over hard spots, until done? Or will he not complete the task because he will lose interest or find it too difficult?

These indications of task commitment do not always apply to other areas. A child who can't always complete projects outside school may do fine in school because of the structure provided there. Your child may persist at video games much longer than you would like and learn how to get really high scores. In thinking about your child, take into account commitment to different kinds of tasks.

Task commitment is essential for succeeding independently at computer programming and other computer projects. With it, the child will have the drive to master programming or other projects and will do well on his own or with a limited amount of help. A child with less commitment can also succeed at programming, but will probably need more instruction and more structured practice. You may want to get this child a simpler language, like Pilot, to work in. You will also want to try to keep the size of programming projects manageable so the child can have the feeling of success that comes with completing these tasks.

In areas other than programming, you will want to be sure that some of the activities the child takes on are activities he will complete. This applies even to games. It can take a great deal of time to complete an adventure game or to learn how to win at other video games. There is no harm at all in a child's beginning many projects, learning something from them, and then dropping them, but you and he will probably want to see at least some projects completed for the satisfaction this will give you both.

A child who starts huge building projects with Lego blocks but never completes the projects, might enjoy a building game like Pinball Construction Set where he can quickly build a pinball game on the screen and then play the game. This same child might enjoy creating a city on the screen by programming the graphics in Logo, but you should realize that he might not finish this project either. He *will* learn useful programming skills in the process of trying, however.

Creativity

Another important trait for computer success is creativity or divergent thinking. The creative child will come up with the unexpected answer to a question or the unusual solution to a problem.

Ask yourself whether your child, if confronted with a set of materials like dolls, blocks, or furniture, will use the materials in one way, perhaps insisting that this is the "right way" to use them; or will try out the materials in different ways at different times, perhaps using them in some very unexpected ways. This second pattern shows divergent thinking.

A child whose thinking is divergent will probably be good at games like Boggle where you have to find many ways of reusing and recombining letters. This kind of child may not do well on standardized multiple-choice tests because he will be able to find reasons why more than one answer is correct.

Creativity is particularly helpful in programming because the creative person will find the best way to accomplish a task in programming by being open to trying several different methods. It is also useful for using computer tools like word processors and database systems in innovative ways. A creative child may surprise you by using the computer in an unexpected way. This child may also be good at programming or other computer tasks, especially if he also possesses organization skills and task commitment. The danger is that the creative child may try out so many solutions at once that he never settles on one way of approaching a problem.

A less creative child (whose thinking is characterized as convergent instead of divergent) may need more help in programming to be able to see a new solution to a programming problem or to learn new techniques. On the other hand, this child may find it easier to learn some of the rather arbitrary rules of programming, accepting that certain things just have to be done in a certain way. The creative child may need help with this.

If you are interested in fostering creativity in your child, you might consider having the child try out such software as adventure games and programs like Facemaker that actually encourage and reward divergent thinking, as well as artistic tools such as Paint and Painter Power.

Verbal Versus Spatial Abilities

Some children are better at verbal skills; some at spatial skills. There has been much talk in recent years of left-brain/right-brain dominance, but we're not trying to make a correlation to this, because that issue is complex and easily misinterpreted. We're simply recognizing that some children are better at getting information from verbal material and some from charts or diagrams. Some have more facility with words; some with objects, maps, drawings, and so forth.

Ask yourself, if my child needs to do a task where he needs instruction (baking a cake, installing a bicycle light, etc.), will he prefer to read instructions; or will he look at diagrams and pictures? The first pattern shows verbal orientation.

Ask yourself also, is my child better at reading books or at tasks like reading a map or building complicated structures? This will also give you a clue to your child's orientation.

There is nothing wrong with a child who is better at either verbal or spatial tasks, but you should take this orientation into account when thinking about the kinds of computer tasks and the kinds of computer software you want for your child. Because a personal computer is both a graphics tool and a language tool, it works well for both types of children.

Never mind the TV-like screen and flashy graphics of the

personal computer. In reality, the computer culture is one in which there are vast quantities of written material to be absorbed. The child who is better at verbal tasks will have an easier time with computer books, computer magazines, and the instructions that come with hardware and software than the child weaker in these skills. The child who is better at spatial tasks will need more help from you in handling all this written information. You may want to look for software that requires less reading. Check the amount of printed instruction that comes with the software and also preview the level and amount of written instructions that appear on the screen before you buy.

For a child who, for example, is having trouble with math and is better at spatial than verbal tasks, don't buy a math tutorial that explains every concept in text on the screen. Look instead for software where the instruction is more visual, where the screen shows graphic examples of concepts.

On the other hand, the child who is better at spatial tasks will probably do very well at video games, including educational software set in a video game format. Such software is often designed to require some spatial skills, and a child who is better at spatial tasks can probably handle this software very well. An example of this kind of software is a math drill where you have to solve a problem coming at you on an invading spaceship, move your laser gun to the right spot, and fire the gun to blow up the invader. You can't succeed unless you can both solve the problem and fire the gun properly, which requires some quick judgments about movement on the screen as well as good hand-eye coordination. You might want to avoid this kind of software for a child without good spatial skills unless it is possible to slow the speed of the program down to the point where he can handle it.

Some software can help a child to get better at spatial tasks. One example of this kind of software is The Factory game from Sunburst where you line up a series of make-believe machines on the computer screen to create a "product" with holes and lines punched in a certain pattern. It requires good spatial orientation and the ability to picture the results of actions. Because you get feedback by seeing the product created by your machine, you can learn these skills while playing the game.

Need for Feedback and External Reinforcement

Some children have a great need to be told that what they are doing is correct or good. In other words, they need a lot of feedback and reassurance. This is the kind of child who shows you every drawing at every stage of its development. This is also the kind of child with whom you have to sit while he is doing his homework, encouraging and praising him so that he will finish the task.

For the child who needs this support, the computer can be ideal. A computer is capable of giving responses to every action a child makes. In a math drill, for example, it can tell the child whether every number he types is correct and then tell him whether the final result is correct. Some software is better than others at giving clear, unambiguous, immediate responses to the child's actions. To find this quality in software, insist on previewing software before you buy. Try it out, getting answers right and wrong at every possible point. Does the computer immediately respond to each thing you type? Does it at least sometimes tell you something more than "Wrong. Try again" by giving you a hint or extra help? Does it reward your correct answers? When you are wrong, can you tell where you made the error? A child who needs support can benefit from this type of feedback.

Impulsive/Reflective Styles

The person whose style is impulsive jumps quickly to a decision; the reflective person considers choices and options carefully before making a decision. You can probably identify your child's style very easily. Both of these traits can be useful when dealing with computers.

The reflective, methodical child will do well on software where he has to read directions carefully in order to use the material correctly. The impulsive child will tend to rush in and try everything without reading, so he will do better with software where the documentation isn't so important. Generally speaking, computer tools like word processing and database systems require more careful study than application programs such as educational games. Nevertheless, some of the newer tool programs provide extensive "Help screens" to assist you in learning while you are working on the computer and to serve as reminders later on. Also, some tools such as those on the Macintosh are designed to encourage experimentation and to reduce the amount of learning needed to operate them.

Using a simulation can be helpful to both types of children. The impulsive child will feel free to try many different numbers or answers rapidly and will quickly go through the full range of the simulation. The reflective child, on the other hand, will be slower to try different options, but will probably think more carefully about the simulation response to each option and may well learn more of the basic concepts underlying the simulation. You can encourage each type of child to try out some of the behavior of the other type. You can ask the impulsive child to think about what principles he is uncovering and to try to predict the effects of commands as he tries them out. You can encourage the reflective child to try some random responses to see what happens and to explore some of the more exotic options and features of the software.

Implications

As you can see from this section, there are a number of personality/learning-style characteristics to keep in mind when choosing software for your child. For every personality type we have discussed, there is appropriate software available. To choose it correctly, you must first accurately recognize your child's personality. It should also be clear that you'll need to preview software before you buy and make some judgments based on what you see on the screen. Insightful reviews of software in computer magazines and newspapers can also help.

AGE AND SEX

Girls and Boys and Computers

Almost everyone who has observed girls and boys working with computers has noticed the same thing: Although girls and boys can be equally proficient at working with computers, it is boys who seem particularly interested in computers. With younger children, few differences are seen, but by the fifth grade or so, boys dominate the computer clubs, the computer room, and the school computer culture. This trend continues right up through adulthood. A disproportionate number of men are found in computer clubs and computer-related occupations.

What is the reason for this? It appears to have something to do with math anxiety, which is a greater problem for girls than boys. Computers tend to be seen—incorrectly—as math machines, and children who don't like math sometimes shy away from them. Another factor may be the prevalence of games with themes that appeal more to boys—space, war games, shooting, etc. (Most games are developed by male programmers.) And perhaps it is also because computers are a very advanced kind of technology, and traditionally in our society, technology has been the province of men. Because boys tend to dominate the computer room at school, it's easy for girls taking computer courses or interested in computers to feel uncomfortable about even going into the room to do some work.

Whatever the source of the problem, there are ways to overcome a girl's computer phobia or keep it from developing in the first place. One way is to buy your daughter a home computer. An interesting study done in Princeton, New Jersey, compared girls' and boys' progress in a programming course. The girls and boys had the same instruction and the same access to computer time to practice after school. While we should be careful not to overgeneralize from this one study, it is interesting that, while boys did better than girls in the course, the boys' success was correlated with time spent practicing in the computer center after school. Very few girls used the computer center after school. The girls who used a home computer for extra practice at home did better than other girls in the course. The best way to learn to program is to practice the skill, and, apparently, girls often feel more comfortable doing that practice at home than in the school's computer center.

In addition to providing a computer for your daughter, you can look for games and educational software that have themes she is comfortable with. Earlier we mentioned software for girls from Rhiannon software. There are many other software packages not specifically designed for girls that nonetheless have themes that girls respond to well.

If your daughter dislikes math, you can avoid increasing her math anxiety or associating it with computers by not making math the first activity she does on the computer. If you enroll her in a computer class, make sure that the class does not emphasize mathematical uses for programming. It should teach handling of words or graphics before handling of numbers. The same thing applies to any software programming tutorials or books that you buy her.

Attitude and example play a large role also. It could help if your children see that their mother and father are both interested in computers and that neither regards computers as belonging to the other sex.

Age

As we saw in Chapter 2, children of different ages can use computers in different ways. There are natural stages of development in terms of which types of computer tasks children can handle and want to become involved in at different ages. You should keep these differences in mind when thinking about the kinds of things your child might do with a computer and when you're picking out software as well.

However, keep in mind that computers will often enable children to do and learn things they ordinarily wouldn't be ready for. A computer can make abstract concepts very concrete, thus allowing a child who can't yet handle abstract reasoning to grasp the concept. Turtle graphics are an interesting illustration of this principle. With turtle graphics, young children handle some very sophisticated geometric concepts concerning angles and rotation that they probably couldn't learn in the abstract. Seeing the turtle moving on the screen in response to their commands makes the geometric principles concrete and puts them within their grasp.

The computer can also make potentially difficult tasks interesting and easy enough so a younger child will attempt them. Children who wouldn't have the skills or knowledge necessary to set up a science experiment can use a science simulation. Many children will attempt to spell words that are beyond their level in school, just so they can do an interesting word game. With the feedback they get from the computer, they will learn to spell some of them. Many young children learn to type with typing games, even though, traditionally, typing is not taught before the eighth or ninth grade.

SPECIAL NEEDS

If your child has a learning disability or a physical disability, you will need to take some steps to be sure that he can use the computer comfortably. In the case of a learning disability, working with the teacher or specialist at your child's school is probably the best way to make sure that the activities you pick are both reasonable and beneficial to your child.

Motor Impairments

For a child with motor impairments that affect the ability to use the keyboard of a computer, you should consider getting a special keyboard. Most computers allow you to hook up a keyboard different from the one that comes with the computer or to add an additional keyboard. One keyboard, the Presto Digitizer from Innovation in Palo Alto, California, allows you to use the Apple or PET computer via a stylus and a small pad. Other keyboards have large, well-separated keys. Even an inexpensive graphics tablet could be used by some children because touching different parts of the surface sends information to the computer and allows the pad to be used as an input device for multiple choice situations.

Other approaches for motor-impaired children include: overlay cutouts that create a recessed hole for each key, allowing the child to zero in on it without brushing the wrong key; for a child using one finger or a mouthstick, special reassignment of "control" and "shift" keys so that they can be typed sequentially rather than simultaneously with other keys; and special software and signaling devices that select letters or other choices from a moving display on the screen.

There also are ways to reduce the amount of routine typing the child must do to execute sequences of commands or to enter hard-to-type words during word processing. These methods involve the use of programmable function keys and special software (such as ProKey for the IBM PC) that allow you to cause a pre-assigned sequence of commands or words to be typed in automatically whenever you press a given function key. (These methods apply equally well to children without handicaps and can be real time-savers.)

Speech control of the computer is another possibility. A number of devices convert speech to commands the computer can understand. One of these, the Voice Input Module from Voice Machine Communications of Santa Ana, California, can be used with many applications on the Apple computer and has the ability to recognize almost any voice. If your child has a speech impairment as well, you should be careful that the voice input device you buy will be able to learn your child's speech.

A good deal of software can be easily adapted for use with a simple input key (usually a button or pedal). Some of this adaptation has already been done by the software publishers.

Blind or Visually Impaired Children

For those children with partial sight, two devices in particular can be helpful. These devices, the VisualTek and the Apollo, both take text from the computer and enlarge it many times on a special monitor. The VisualTek connects directly with an Apple or an IBM PC; the Apollo connects via a modem to some personal computers. (More elaborate versions of these two devices can be used with printed material as well, on a split screen. A closed-circuit TV camera is used to put the printed material on the screen. An optional motorized platform moves the printed material around easily and quickly.)

For some visually impaired children, software developed to use the Mockingboard speech synthesizer might be appropriate. The Mockingboard produces very clear synthesized speech. Its use varies with the software, but it might provide some extra help for a child who has some difficulty reading a computer screen.

Some companies have developed generalized speech output that will work with many software programs. PC Speak (for the IBM PC) and PC Speakjr (for the IBM PCjr) are software programs ($200–$400) from Solution by Example (P.O. Box 307, New Town Branch, Boston, MA 02258) that send text appearing on the screen to a voice synthesizer to be spoken. They allow you to stop and go back to review other parts of the screen as well. This software can be used with synthesizers that vary widely in cost and sound quality. These include the low-cost Votrax and Echo products ($200–$400) and the high-cost Speech-Plus product ($2750). If your child is interested in the Apple, you could investigate a series of packages from Science Products for the Blind that combine the (Apple-compatible) Franklin Ace computer with an Echo II speech synthesizer and also let the child know if the SHIFT LOCK is activated and which disk drive is in use, helpful features to a programmer. Prices for the total package, including computer, range from $1500–$2000. (Write Box A, Southeastern, PA 19399.)

Braille output is also available for personal computers. For example, a device called the VersaBraille (TeleSensory, Inc., Palo Alto, California) interfaces with the Apple computer and produces "soft-copy" braille on a retractable metal-pin display that furnishes one line at a time in braille. It also can be used to record and retrieve information either in braille or voice recording on cassettes. The cost of these devices is usually quite high. However, they are available in the computer labs of some colleges, and your child could learn to use a computer in the lab even if it's not practical to have a computer at home. You might also request that your local school system purchase such equipment.

Children with Hearing Impairments

Because personal computers are primarily visual- rather than audio-based devices, they present few obstacles to children with hearing impairments. In fact, children with hearing impairments can take advantage of personal computers to overcome other communications obstacles they may have, primarily by using modems to communicate over phone lines with friends and fellow students. In some geographic areas, there are special networks and electronic bulletin boards to facilitate communication between deaf persons having dissimilar equipment, such as teletypes and personal computers, and to advertise special events of interest to the deaf community.

Hearing-impaired students can also improve their communication skills by using word-processing programs. Programs that check spelling and give feedback on style and grammar could be particularly helpful. Subscriptions to network information services might also be helpful, when they encourage the hearing-impaired student to take an interest in local and world events.

TAILORING THE COMPUTER TO YOUR CHILD

By now you should have a good list of possible computer activities for your child, along with some special requirements to keep in mind when looking at hardware and software. You should spend some time in computer stores and some time looking through computer magazines (see Appendix A) to see just what is available for the activities you have in mind. Take your child along to a computer store and let him try out some of the types of software you think are appropriate. Talk to your child about the activities you think he'd enjoy on the computer.

You might also write to or talk to people in organizations that specialize in the interests that your child wants to pursue (stamp-collecting clubs, ham-radio groups, environmental-protection and ecological organizations, photography clubs, theater groups, etc.) and ask them about special software, hardware, remote databases, and computer newsletters that some of their members are using to pursue their special interests.

Your next step will be to look over information on different computers to see which will help your child to carry out the activities you've selected. You'll be looking for a computer with the hardware features needed to accomplish these tasks. In the next chapter, we'll tell you which features your child will need.

CHAPTER 5

Selecting Your Child's Computer

PUTTING IT ALL TOGETHER

Now that you know (or have a better idea of) which computer activities make sense for your child, you have to find the computer hardware and software that have the features your child needs most. This chapter will explain how to do this.

Before we discuss how to match computer features to activities, we will go over some basic considerations of computer cost—usually a very important topic to parents. Then we'll describe how you can select the right computer for your child. We'll give examples of common computer activities and the computer features that are necessary to support those activities, and we'll present charts that compare these features on different computers. You'll be able to see which computers have the features that are appropriate for your child. Finally, we'll give you some help in narrowing down your choice to one computer.

THE SYSTEM APPROACH

Systems

A *system* is a set of parts that work together to accomplish a task. In a computer system, the CPU, memory, software, and peripherals can all work together to do, for example, word processing or graphics. In the past, most people tended to buy computers rather than systems, and that is how the computer companies sold their machines. But everyone discovered that just buying a computer was not enough. It was also necessary to buy peripherals and software. In response to this need, some computer companies have started to offer systems to their customers. They package a set of hardware (such as a computer, disk drive, and monitor) and sometimes even include software (for example, word-processing software) in the package. A computer like the Coleco Adam is a perfect example of this. The company sells the computer, a storage device, a letter-quality printer, and built-in word processing software together.

In general, you should think about buying a computer system, not just a computer. You can either buy a packaged system or you can put one together yourself by buying all the components you need from one manufacturer or a number of manufacturers. A rule of thumb is that disk drives are usually bought from the primary computer manufacturer, and printers and software are usually bought from someone else.

Not everyone needs a system, however. If you are buying a computer so that your child can do some fairly simple programming tasks and play a few cartridge games, you can probably buy a computer rather than a computer system.

Prices

For most parents, price is a major consideration in buying a computer for a child. Parents do differ, however, in what they consider a reasonable level of expense for their child. Typically, parents will want to spend less for a younger child, but their ideas of "less" will differ as well. You probably have a general idea of how much you want to spend, but in setting your final budget, take into consideration a few factors.

First, in deciding on an expense level, see how much computing power you'll be able to buy for the money. It may be worth it to spend a little more if that amount of money will make the computer you buy a much more useful and powerful machine. For example, if you're thinking of spending up to $500, look to see what you could get for over $500 as well. You might find a computer that supports a wider range of activities that might help your child now and in the future.

Also bear in mind the cost of the entire system that you will eventually want to have. If you plan for the purchase of a system, you'll see what the whole package is going to cost you. Otherwise, you might buy a computer because it's inexpensive, and then find a few months later when you decide to add the disk drive, that the drives for that computer are very expensive and that your bargain isn't such a bargain anymore.

In thinking about your purchase, bear in mind that it's probably true that your child will use this computer or computer system for about two to three years. Then you might be able to upgrade your system in a fairly substantial way to accommodate your child's new needs. Or you might want to buy a new system that will be on the market at that time. Because of the trends in the computer market, prices will be lower, especially for peripherals. New devices, new concepts, and new software will be available and you may want to take advantage of them.

Paradoxically, this is a good argument for buying a system now and not waiting. You will never get to a point where you can say that no more computer innovations will be made; your computer will always become outdated. So if you find a computer that meets your child's needs, by all means buy it now and be prepared for a replacement in a few years. Your added experience will also help you make a better selection among the choices that will be available at that time.

You might even consider establishing a special savings account to be used for future purchases of personal computer software and add-ons and for system replacement. Each year you would put in an amount of money and then periodically draw out amounts as your child's needs change and you want to make a purchase. This type of planning may be the most realistic approach in the long run.

The potential exists for financial service companies to aid in this process by designing special investment funds that are accompanied by "upgrade or replacement" contracts. When and whether such programs will emerge is an open question, but the logic of the market needs leads us to predict that it will occur in the next five years.

If you are making a fairly substantial investment now and don't like the idea of starting over with a new system in a few years, then look for a system that will be expandable and adaptable in the future. Some systems are fixed; some are flexible. The sign of a flexible system is the presence of expansion "slots" or areas in the computer where you can add ROM chips or boards to accomplish new tasks. (The advertisement or salesperson will usually tell you this; you don't have to look inside the machine.) The Apple IIe, for example, has a series of empty slots on the main logic board of the computer itself. Into those slots you can plug ROM cards to control disks or printers; to include a different CPU that runs a different operating system like CP/M; to use special graphics chips, clock devices, extra memory, etc. The IBM PC also has slots to add peripherals. Another sign of a flexible system is more "ports," outlets where you can plug, for example, RS–232 cables and other communication cables and devices. These plugs, and the internal circuits that support them inside the machine, make it possible to add such peripherals as printers, modems, robots, etc. (Some newer computers, such as the Mindset and the Sinclair QL, have a more elaborate system of ports on the outside that is designed to allow a sequence of modular expansion steps.)

Certain features are simply not available on computer systems that cost only a few hundred dollars. These include the ability to run a sophisticated operating system (such as CP/M, MS-DOS, or UNIX) and the ability to produce an eighty-column display on the screen. Currently, in most cases, if the computer costs less than $500, these features are not available at all; if the computer costs between $500 and $1000, one or both of these features are available, often as options; if the computer costs more than $1000, these are probably standard features. Disk drives and printers also add to the cost of a system, but there is more variation in these prices. They may be available on even the least expensive systems.

PATH TO A DECISION

From Chapter 4 you have a list of activities that your child might engage in with a computer and an idea of the special ways the activities should be tailored to your child's needs. The first step in deciding which computer to buy is to identify the computer features your child needs to facilitate these activities. If you made a chart, you can put this information under "Software/Hardware." Some of the features will be hardware features, some software. Discuss them with your child to be sure you agree on these features.

Next, look at specific computers in your price range (and at some higher and lower priced systems) to see which ones have the features you want. The charts in Appendix B will help you here. You'll be looking for systems that have all or most of the features your child needs. Also look for software for these computers.

Once you've found systems that meet all or some of your needs, decide what the trade-offs are. Which features are really important to your child? Which features can you live with in a modified form?

Take into account some other factors like who else will be using the system, the computer your child has available at school, and so forth.

Try out the computer systems you have in mind, and then make a decision on a purchase and an approach to future upgrades.

One Family's Experience

Here is how one family picked a computer as a gift for their twelve-year-old son's birthday. They recognized that their son was a bright child who was not very interested in school and who was not realizing his potential in any activity. He was taking a computer course on Saturdays, and, while learning programming there, became interested in computer game graphics. The parents felt that the excitement of having a computer on which he could design his own graphics would motivate him to work hard on this new interest, so they identified computer graphics as an activity for their son.

They decided that they needed a computer in the middle-price range that had good, easy-to-use graphics so their child wouldn't become discouraged. They planned to buy a color TV to go with the computer and one disk drive as well, for quicker access to the programs their son wrote. Once they had located several computer systems where the total price would be within their price range, they picked one that was also used at their child's school so that he could get the benefit of help from the computer teacher and, perhaps later, take classes.

ACTIVITIES AND FEATURES

Let's look at some of the more popular computer activities and the hardware/software features needed for each activity. We can't describe every possible activity, but from the examples, you should develop the ability to match features to activities.

The first activity we'll discuss is word processing. This very popular computer activity can be carried out at a very simple level or at a complex level. At the simple level, we're thinking of a case where the tasks the child does are not very sophisticated and the written material produced is not very long. For example, an eight-year-old writing stories and poems, and a ten-year-old writing plays and doing short written assignments, are using the word processor at a fairly simple level. At the complex level, we're thinking of a college student or high-school student writing long papers, for example, a thirteen-year-old doing reports on science experiments with lots of tabular material or a high school student writing elaborate term papers. Obviously, many children fall in between these two groups, but they will be closer to one or the other.

Word Processing—Simple Level

What you see—Although it is possible to do simple word processing with fewer than forty characters across on the screen, it is probably not a good idea to go lower than thirty-two characters across.

Either a TV or monitor will work, but for visual clarity and comfort, it may be desirable to have a monitor if your child is doing a great deal of work. Be sure that the picture signal sent by the computer is acceptable in quality, format, and typeface for viewing over long periods of time. Color is not important.

Software—The word-processing software you pick should be inexpensive, or built in, should let your child enter, modify, and print text easily (probably in several typefaces if they are available on your printer), and might also contain some more advanced features like movement of text or searches for words within the text.

Keyboard—One of the better keyboards is desirable. Most computers with small-size keys are not suitable. The IBM PCjr keyboard is borderline. (Its keys are long and narrow and may be difficult to type on for long periods of time, but they do have grooves for the fingers and feel solid.) Preferably, get a keyboard with true full-size, typewriter-style keys, like Coleco, Atari, or Commodore. (Definitely get full-size keys for a touch typist.) Even better is a keyboard with special keys for word-processing functions.

Printer—Your child must have a printer. Dot-matrix is fine, but the printer should print eighty characters across. Type of paper doesn't matter, but ask about the cost of the paper used by the printer. Some inexpensive printers use expensive thermal paper.

Memory and storage—It can be hard to find software for a system with little memory. Even if you can get software, your child will soon want more memory to work on longer documents. Consider 48K or 64K rather than 16K. As for storage, ordinary cassettes will work on some word-processing systems, but their slowness can be annoying. If you can afford it, go with a disk system or high-speed cassettes. A single disk-drive system is fine.

Operating system—There is virtue in a 16-bit system, because of its speed and ability to run newer, more powerful software, but it is not necessary.

Suggestions—The Coleco Adam is designed for word processing and includes a (slow and noisy) letter-quality printer in a very inexpensive packaged system. It also has a typewriter-style keyboard with special keys to help in word processing. Another useful system is an Atari with the AtariWriter software package (available on cartridge) and the inexpensive Atari 1027 letter-quality printer, which is quieter and faster than the Coleco printer. There is also the popular Bank Street Writer (intended for students of junior-high age and up) that runs on the Apple IIe and the Commodore 64, among others. The IBM PCjr using a program like HomeWord or Bank Street Writer might be a choice, but the keyboard is the minimum acceptable.

The Commodore VIC might be the choice for a very young child, bearing in mind the slowness of the cassette storage method and the very narrow text display. Still, it might work for simple uses, and it is inexpensive. A useful software package for VIC is the Quick Brown Fox, which has the virtues of producing a wider text display and loading from cartridge rather than cassette. (The text your child writes must still be stored on cassette.) Another good choice would be the Commodore 64 and one of the other word processing software packages available for it. Also consider the Sinclair QL.

Word Processing—Complex Level

What you see—For complex word processing, you should in most cases go with an 80-column text display and a monitor. Bear in mind that an 80-column display is often available on 40-column systems as an upgrade and, if so, you should get it. Your child may be able to do word processing with a 40-column display, but she won't be able to see as much text on the screen or see what the finished product will look like. A 64-column display is adequate.

Software—Look for packages that support more sophisticated word-processing operations like search, advanced formatting, split screen editing, movement of text, footnotes, and if an older child is, for example, an officer in a club, the ability to use the word processor with a mailing list for form letters.

There are two types of word-processing software. In one, you see on the screen the format you'll see on paper—margins, indents, tabs, etc. In the other, you instruct the word processor to do the kind of format you want, but don't see it until you print the text. The latter type allows you more format options

—poetry, lists, etc.—but is harder to use. It is probably better for college-age students than younger ones.

Keyboard—A typewriter-type keyboard is essential. One with so-called function keys is desirable.

Printer—Again, this is essential. A dot-matrix printer is probably fine, although your child might want to get a sample of the print from a computer store to show teachers to see if this will be acceptable to them. A letter-quality printer might be better for some applications. (Sometimes you can make arrangements to use a letter-quality printer in the school's computer lab for final drafts.) Higher speed in printing is a good feature to have when you are printing long documents. A two-speed printer (for draft and correspondence quality) can be very helpful as well.

Memory and storage—The minimum memory for complex word processing is 64K. Storage should be on a disk. Two disks are helpful for making backup copies easily. Larger capacity drives of 300K and up are a good choice.

Operating systems—CP/M and MS-DOS both support sophisticated word processing, but MS-DOS is easier to use and runs on a 16-bit chip. But remember, it is also possible to get good word processing packages without getting a CP/M or MS-DOS system. Good software is available on Apple's regular DOS operating system, for example.

Suggestions—The Acorn with its built-in "View" word processor, eighty-column capabilities, and advanced graphics and music features is an excellent all-around choice. The KayPro with free, very good word-processing software might be a good choice for a college student who doesn't want color or games. It is portable as well. (You might also consider the Seequa Chameleon, a somewhat more expensive portable, which resembles the KayPro but can also run 16-bit MS-DOS programs and has graphics.) The Apple IIe (either using its regular operating system or perhaps upgraded to use CP/M, depending on the software you choose) is a good choice, as is the IBM PC and the Apple Macintosh. For word-processing software, consider The Final Word (a very advanced and logical system that needs large-capacity disk drives and CP/M), WordStar (a popular CP/M program that is somewhat harder to use), Perfect Writer (similar to the Final Word), EasyWriterII, MultiMate, WordPerfect, and Volkswriter, among others.

A family whose high-school student needs a word processor for long papers and whose ten-year-old wants to write short school assignments, should consider buying a rather sophisticated computer, such as the Apple IIe with two disk drives and a monitor. For the older child they could buy a CP/M ROM card, an 80-column card, and a package like WordStar. For the younger child, they could buy the Bank Street Writer software package, which uses Apple's standard operating system and the built-in Apple 40-column display signal on the same monitor. In this way they will get a system that can handle both simple and complex word processing.

The same approach can be taken when a parent is sharing a computer with a younger child. Or they might be able to use the same computer and software. The advantage here is that each user can help the other learn the system and all of its idiosyncrasies by pooling their experience. Good solutions include getting a higher-priced, "user-friendly" computer like the Apple Macintosh or the Epson QX-10 (which have moderately sophisticated but extremely easy-to-use word-processing software) or getting a lower-priced, relatively easy-to-use computer such as the Coleco Adam or the Acorn (which have built-in word processing software in ROM), or the Sinclair QL (which has this software on high-speed tape).

Graphics

There are at least four users of graphics. The first two, who don't do any graphics programming, are the child who "draws" on the computer screen with the aid of a graphics tablet and the child who creates graphics on the screen without using the tablet but with graphics software designed for use without programming (often with the aid of a joystick or arrow keys on the keyboard). There's a great deal of overlap in these two kinds of uses of graphics. Sometimes a child will start doing graphics without a tablet, and after she shows that she likes working with graphics, her parents will invest the extra $100 or so in a graphics tablet. Other children will switch back and forth between the two methods depending on the kinds of effects they can get with each one. (Professional computer-graphic artists do the same thing.)

In deciding which of these two uses fits your child, take age into account. A very young child will do better with a program that shows paint pots on the screen and allows simple drawing with a joystick. A graphics tablet, because of the use of symbols and special rules needed to operate it, is better for an older child.

If your child is very interested in drawing, a tablet will be best for her. Graphics software is best for creating abstract patterns, creating moving patterns, creating animation, and for getting quick results. Less drawing skill is required because typically the purpose is to create interesting effects and to experiment with a new medium.

The next two types of users of graphics do the programming themselves. First is the child who programs simple graphics, perhaps as a way of learning a programming language like BASIC or Logo. The other is the more experienced programmer who creates more elaborate graphics that are to be used in video games or other computer programs.

Each of these four users tends to require slightly different features from a computer system. Keep in mind the way your child will use computer graphics as you read the rest of this section. *Figure 5–1* shows the most important feature(s) for each type of user. Use it as a guide as you read this section and when you select a computer system.

Color—More colors and more shades of color allow greater richness in graphics. When you evaluate a computer, check to see how many colors are available in the higher-resolution modes. A large number of colors is an especially nice feature when a child is using a graphics tablet or software package to create pictures because more colors allow a wider range of artistic expression.

Resolution—A greater number of cells on the screen gives more resolution and greater clarity to the graphics, but your child may well be able to manage without the highest possible resolution. Look at the graphics actually produced by a computer to see if they are adequate in resolution. Resolution is probably most important with a graphics tablet or software. It's also important for complex computer graphics.

Graphics software—Good graphics software packages make it possible to draw and sometimes even animate on the computer screen. For example, there are packages available for the Apple, like Painter Power or Magic Paintbrush, that make it possible to create pictures on the screen. Painter Power allows the user to create full screen patterns of colors that move and change as the game paddle is moved. It would be very difficult to create such art by programming. Nor would it be possible to create this art with a graphics tablet. Magic Paintbrush and others allow the child to do pictures more like those done with a graphics tablet. The pictures can be abstract or more realistic, depending on the artist. Be sure graphics software packages are available for the computer you buy if your child will be doing this kind of activity.

FIGURE 5–1 / **Important Features for Different Graphics Users**

	Color & Resolution	Graphics Utilities	Graphics Software	Ease of Graphics Programming
Child who does art with a graphics tablet	X		*	Not applicable
Child who does art with software designed for use without programming	X		X	Not applicable
Child who does simple graphics, often as an aid to learning programming				X
Child who does complex graphics programming	X	X		

* Tablets usually include software to help the child use the tablet.

Graphics utilities—Some graphics software packages are designed to help the programmer rather than the nonprogrammer. These "graphics utilities" facilitate the use of graphics, making it easier to create shapes or pictures that are then used in the child's own program. This feature is useful if your child is programming a game with graphics. Using shapes and pictures created by this kind of graphics utility can be a little tricky. Often you have to understand how the computer stores things in memory in order to retrieve your art from the computer's memory when running your program. Read the manual before you buy to see how difficult it is to use the package in the first place and how difficult it is to use the art in a program.

Ease of use—When you are *programming* graphics, the ease of creating graphics differs on different computers. For a child learning programming via graphics, this can be a very important factor. It's also helpful for the more experienced programmer to have graphics that are easier to use.

One reason that programming graphics is hard is that you have to specify what you want drawn on the screen by using a coordinate system. Each location on the screen has an X and a Y coordinate location. Typically, a younger child will never have been exposed to a formal coordinate system before. Once a child has picked up the coordinate system concept, she has to be able to use it to describe the kinds of lines and curves she wants drawn. Some systems make this easier than others. The TRS-80 Color Computer, for example, has commands to let you draw circles and squares without specifying all the coordinates and also lets you color them in easily. The Commodore 64 graphics are harder to use without the Simon's BASIC cartridge and its special graphics commands.

Looking through the manuals that come with the computers and the books on that computer's graphics in a computer store or bookstore should give you a feeling for the machine's ease of use. The graphics are probably easy to use *if:* the books use a fairly small number of commands when discussing the machine's graphics; don't refer to any "assembly language" programming; don't contain the commands "PEEK" or "POKE" (ways of looking at what is stored in memory or altering it); do show commands like "CIRCLE" or "FILL" to let you do a whole operation with one command. Talking to someone who uses the machine for graphics can also help you make your decision.

Generally speaking, low-resolution graphics and character-set graphics (remember, these character-set graphics are shapes put together to make a picture as in *Figure 3–6)* are easier for a novice programmer to use. So if you are looking for simple graphics, look for low-resolution graphics with lots of colors. Because low-resolution is defined differently on different computers, you can also look for a greater number of cells in the low-resolution system you pick. Also look for character-set graphics with an assortment of shapes to use to build pictures. For example, Atari's character-set graphics are quite easy to use, while their low- and high-resolution graphics are more difficult.

For many children, Logo turtle graphics will be the easiest graphics system to use. The Logo language is designed to facilitate graphics, whereas, in languages like BASIC, graphics commands are a kind of add-on and require more sophistication to use. Turtle graphics are also available in some Pilot languages; Pilot is also an easy-to-learn language.

In turtle graphics, the child directs a tiny "turtle" on the screen to draw. Rather than using a coordinate system, the child commands the turtle to move forward a certain distance, turn a certain number of degrees, go forward again, etc. As the turtle moves, it leaves a trail behind it in a color selected by the child, thus drawing a picture. The child can create patterns for the turtle to draw, like circles, squares, or parts of pictures, give the pattern a name, and then get the turtle to recreate that pattern by using the name as a command. Using turtle graphics teaches a child some fairly sophisticated concepts in geometry and also in computer programming.

One more note on graphics. It's useful, as well, to be able to mix text and graphics on the same screen, but many computers don't allow you to do this or allow text only in the bottom four lines of the screen. If your child wants to label drawings or graphs or otherwise freely mix text and graphics, look either for a computer that allows this or a graphics utility package that allows it.

Animation—Computers differ in their animation capabilities. Some, like the Atari computers, have what is called "player-missile" graphics, which allow you to move objects around the screen smoothly. (The term comes from video games that use players on the screen and missiles such as basketballs or rockets.) Some computers have "sprites" which can be used for animation. A sprite is an invisible point whose screen location can be made to change. Each sprite can be assigned its own object or shape to carry around. Moving the sprite causes the shape to move. A single object or groups of objects can be made to dance around the screen or move in other patterns. Other computers accomplish animation in other ways, and the quality of animation varies from computer to computer.

Animation is usually the most difficult graphics activity to do on a computer. Atari's animation is very powerful but difficult to use. Even with a graphics utility package like Graphics Magician, animation is not all that easy on the Apple. Sprites are available on a number of computers and are fairly easy to use. The Coleco Adam has 32 sprites.

Your child's requirements for complexity in animation will differ depending on how sophisticated her plans are. A child using software packages or a graphics tablet may not need to worry about animation at all. Animation done with character-set graphics (simply printing your graphics characters in different places on the screen) may be sufficient for a child just learning programming. Or your child may require the most elaborate animation. But if your child is planning to write video games requiring these elaborate types of animation, be sure that she really has the programming skills to do it. Otherwise, you may by buying graphics capabilities that your child can't use. (They will be used by the professional programmers of video games you purchase for the computer, however, and their contribution to the quality of video games may be reason enough to have them.)

Screen—Either a color TV or a color monitor will work for graphics. You will get sharper graphics on the monitor. An "RGB"[1] monitor will give the best color of all, but be sure it will work with your computer. It will be more expensive too.

Keyboard/joysticks—If you're programming graphics, a typewriter keyboard is desirable, but the keyboard is less important

---

[1] In an RGB monitor, there is a separate "gun" for the colors red, green, and blue.

if you're only using graphics packages. A joystick or game paddle is used by some packages to help you draw on the screen.

Graphics tablet—Graphics tablets are available for many computers, often from another manufacturer. The KoalaPad, for example, is available for a number of computers and comes with software to let your child draw, fill in areas with color, erase, copy part of the drawing, and save the results.

Printer—If your child wants a "hard copy" of what she draws, a printer with the capability of printing graphics is a nice addition. Many of the dot-matrix printers will reproduce what is on the screen. Some print in color as well.

Memory—Memory can be critical for graphics. In general, graphics, especially high-resolution graphics, take up a lot of space in memory. So do graphics tablets and much graphics software. If your child will be doing more elaborate graphics than character-set or low-resolution graphics, buy a system with 48K or more memory.

Storage—A disk system is not as crucial for graphics as it is for word processing, but it will speed up the loading of graphics. If you buy a cassette-based computer system, be sure the graphics packages your child wants are available on cassette or cartridge.

Languages—Again, Logo and some versions of PILOT offer turtle graphics. Most BASICs allow graphics programming. A sophisticated graphics programmer will use the assembly language on the computer in preference to any of these high-level languages.

Suggestions—The Atari computers have excellent graphics, which vary in complexity, depending on the type of graphics used. Atari would be a good choice for any of the types of users we have described. For a child who wants to, and has the ability to, program video games, Atari would be a good choice, as it would be for a child who wants to learn programming by character-set graphics. The child could move up to the more sophisticated capabilities as she learns programming. The Atari with a program like Paint would be good for a young child who wants to draw on the computer without a graphics tablet, and it would be equally good with a graphics tablet, such as the Touch Tablet.

The Mindset computer has superb graphics that can be used by the graphics user who creates graphics with software, with a "mouse," or with a graphics tablet. It also allows the sophisticated graphics programmer to program graphics and animation in BASIC with a simplified command set to make the task easier. The $2700 price, which includes an RGB monitor, will probably scare off parents of younger children or those who are not serious about graphics, but it should be given consideration by a parent whose child is serious about computer graphics. This computer can also be used by the parents as a "substitute" IBM PC for word processing, etc.

Apple graphics capabilities are somewhat limited in terms of resolution and color, but the availability of a very large number of graphics software packages for the nonprogrammer and graphics utilities for the programmer makes it a good possibility.

The Acorn graphics are excellent, with very high resolution. They can be programmed by a beginner or an expert, through BASIC.

The TRS-80 Color Computer would be easy for a younger child to program, as would the Commodore 64 with Logo.

For a child who wants to use a graphics tablet, the Commodore 64 or IBM PCjr with a graphics tablet might be a good choice.

For a nine-year-old who likes to draw and who wants to learn programming, one choice is the Commodore 64 with Logo, so she can draw with that language and learn some programming at the same time. She might also use an Atari with either Logo or BASIC (using Atari's character-set graphics). Cassette storage will be adequate for her needs now. Her parents can either let her use a color TV or buy the Commodore color monitor (for either computer), which gives very good images.

Programming

As with word processing and graphics, programming can be approached at several levels. An eight-year-old who wants to learn to write programs, a twelve-year-old who wants to program games, and a college-bound student planning to take computer science have very different needs.

What you see—It's hard to read a program of any complexity on the screen with a display of less than 32 characters across. Color capability and a color TV or monitor are important if the child is programming graphics and games, but not important for other types of programs. To avoid eyestrain for a child who will be spending a great deal of time at the computer, a monitor is highly desirable.

Keyboard—Bear in mind that typing is involved in programming, and get a keyboard that your child is comfortable typing on.

Printer—A printer is essential for programming at the higher end of the programming spectrum, to look over, debug, and revise lengthy programs. A printer is not necessary (although certainly useful) at the lower end. A dot-matrix printer is fine.

Memory—At the high end, more memory is essential (48K and up); at the low end, a lot of memory is not necessary unless your child will be doing graphics programming.

Storage—Cassettes are fine at the low end; disks very desirable at the high end.

Operating systems—At the high end of the programming spectrum, your child should have access to operating systems like CP/M, MS-DOS, or UNIX, at least as an option or upgrade.

Languages—You should give some consideration to the language(s) that will be available on the machine you pick. BASIC is always available for even the lowest priced computers; Logo is often available as well, as are Pascal and PILOT. Other languages may be available as options. Which of these languages your child needs depends on her age, programming knowledge, and goals.

There is some controversy about which language is best for the beginner. Although BASIC is typically taught in most programming courses because it is easy to learn, some educators think that Logo or Pascal are better choices for an introductory computer language. This is because these languages use more sophisticated programming concepts than BASIC and have a clearer "structure" (require more careful advance planning and result in a cleaner and more visible logic). Thus they help the beginner develop better programming habits and a better understanding of programming.

Evidence of the increasing importance of Pascal is the fact that the Educational Testing Service has designated it as the first computer language for which an "Advanced Placement" examination for college credit will be offered. This is because of Pascal's perceived richness in good programming concepts and constructs, which form the basis for the test questions.

Our view is that if your seven- to eleven-year-old child is just beginning to play around with programming and to write some simple programs, either Logo or BASIC is perfectly acceptable as a language. For a younger child, the turtle graphics of PILOT or Logo will be easier to grasp.

For the child eleven and up, again we think either BASIC or Logo is an acceptable first language. If you want your child to get a richer exposure to computer concepts or if your child is interested in a career in computer science, then you should be sure that she is exposed, later on, to sophisticated, "structured" BASIC programming (in a course or book that teaches BASIC with a structured approach), to advanced applications of Logo (not just turtle graphics but programs using the sophisticated features of the language), to Pascal, or to other more advanced languages.

For a student with a serious interest in computer science, one who probably knows at least one language already, it's important to pick a computer that has BASIC, Pascal, and at least one other language from this group: FORTH, LISP, the C language, FORTRAN, APL, Ada, and COBOL. FORTH is becoming a very popular language because of its flexibility. LISP is important for artificial intelligence and "natural language" processing. C is a highly "structured" language, useful for acquiring sophisticated programming concepts. The last four languages mentioned—FORTRAN, APL, Ada, and COBOL— are used on larger minicomputers and mainframe computers. They would be most useful for a student planning to use those computers as well. *Figure 5–2* summarizes this information.

Languages like BASIC are likely to change in the next few years to better reflect both good design principles and the changing needs of today's computer world. In the long-range future, computer languages and operating systems are proba-

FIGURE 5-2 / **Personal Computer Languages**

Language	Comments
Easy to Use	
BASIC	Easy to learn. Simple and all-purpose. Relatively slow. Not structured.
Logo	Easier than BASIC for young children, yet incorporates advanced concepts. Includes Turtle Graphics for drawing. Structured design.
PILOT	Simple "authoring" language for writing educational programs and adventure games. Presents questions, analyzes responses. Often includes graphics.
Advanced	
Pascal	Modular and structured. Fast. Important in computer science education. Sometimes used to design "internal" programs and computer languages.
FORTH	Flexible and extendable. Easily incorporates new features and terms. Fast.
LISP	Widely used in artificial intelligence programs and research. Versions for microcomputers include INTERLISP and MU-LISP
C	Powerful structured language for minicomputers. Often associated with UNIX. Subset versions available for microcomputers.
Large-Computer Languages	
FORTRAN	Widely used in science, social science, and statistical work.
COBOL	Widely used in business.
APL	Sophisticated language for both science and business. Very compact. Uses many mathematical symbols.
Ada	Important new structured language for science and business. Contains many levels of sophistication and many advanced features. Adopted as official language by Department of Defense.

bly going to incorporate more sensitivity and flexibility as broader and younger groups of the population become routine computer users and programmers. This is an exciting frontier that should make computers easier for everyone to use at every age.

Suggestions—At the higher end of the spectrum, CP/M and MS-DOS computer systems tend to support many languages. For example, the IBM PC (or a "compatible"), the Apple IIe with CP/M, and the HP–150 from Hewlett-Packard are good choices for advanced programming. Use of UNIX will also become important.

At the lower end of the spectrum, any system with Logo—for example, the Commodore 64—is a good choice. For simple programming in BASIC, the TRS-80 Color Computer with Extended BASIC is a reasonable choice, although the thirty-two character screen is a limitation. Atari with the Microsoft BASIC cartridge or the Apple IIe (with its own operating system, not CP/M) are very good choices. The Sinclair QL is also a possible choice.

For a high-school student planning to go away to college next year to study electrical engineering and computer design, a family might consider an IBM PC with 256K of memory, amber monitor, two disk drives, dot-matrix printer, modem, and a number of optional languages, including Pascal, C, and FORTRAN.

For a junior-high student just beginning to study BASIC at school, one family bought an Atari with a cassette player for storage. They will buy a disk drive and printer later if their son shows real interest in programming.

Music

Again, there is a range of possible activities in music. Your child may want to play a little music as sound effects in a game, compose songs, or play a performance-quality music synthesizer. Your child may be playing on a piano-like keyboard to produce music or entering her instructions to the computer through the regular computer keyboard, storing those instructions, and listening to the computer play what she composed.

What you hear—The number of "voices" available on the machine and the range of the voices is a critical factor to consider in picking a computer for music. The more voices available, the richer the chords produced and the more interesting the music will be. There are variations among the different brands in the number of voices available and the ease of using them. You should be aware that it is possible to expand the music capabilities of some computers, like the Apple, by purchasing additional music "boards." Some computers also offer the ability to distort the quality of sound, which will be useful for your child if she wants to use sound effects in video games. These sound types are also referred to as "waveform types."

Other computers let you specify what are known as "attack/ decay" and "sustain/release" rates (ADSR for short, and also referred to as the "waveform envelope"), which make the voice sound like different instruments. This is an advanced feature and is very desirable. It gives you the ability to hear music as if it were being played by different instruments such as violin, piano, or saxophone. This ability systematically to change the acoustical characteristics of the sound means that a child can even create imaginary new musical instruments with unique properties. And by working with several voices or by recording multiple tracks, the child can hear several instruments playing at one time.

Computers that offer the built-in ADSR synthesizer feature include the Commodore 64 and the Acorn. The Acorn synthesizer gives you much more elaborate control over the waveform envelope (the sound dynamics) than does the Commodore, and it allows you to specify musical notes and envelope characteristics with simple BASIC commands. However, the Commodore is much less expensive. Other computers such as Apple or IBM can be given this feature with special boards from third party manufacturers.

Software—When your child is composing and storing music without using a synthesizer with a piano-like keyboard (in the majority of cases, this is probably how your child will start out), she'll need music software. As with graphics, your child can make music with a music software package or program it herself. If your child is not learning to program, then look for a software package that will show notes on the screen, let her pick the pitch, volume, and duration of each note, and store and edit the completed song. Even if your child will be learning programming, she'll probably find that this kind of software makes creating music much easier.

Languages—If your child wants to do at least some programming to create music, look for a BASIC where the sound and music commands are easy to use. As with graphics, there is variation in how simple it is to use the BASIC commands to program music. The Commodore 64, for example, is hard to program without Simon's BASIC or special sound software (such as MusiCalc). Atari and the Radio Shack Color Computer both have easy-to-use BASIC music commands; Apple does not. Music programming is easier if the BASIC has commands that let you specify a voice, musical pitch, duration, loudness, etc., usually all in one command. Otherwise, separate POKE statements must be written for each piece of information, which is indirect, tedious, and time-consuming.

Keyboard and synthesizer—For performing music, a piano-like keyboard and synthesizer are necessary. These may be provided by a third-party manufacturer or by the computer company itself. If your child is a good musician with a real interest in synthesized music, or simply wants to explore musical sound seriously and in depth, then it may be worth it to you to buy a keyboard synthesizer and software that allows the user to define the acoustical characteristics of the sounds to be made (even if the computer by itself doesn't have this capability), record multiple tracks, and control the sounds produced in other ways.

One very popular synthesizer is the alphaSyntauri for the Apple IIe computer. It will produce good synthesized music, allowing your child to compose, play, and record up to sixteen tracks. The system also includes optional software to help teach sight-reading and to print sheet music directly from keyboard notes that were played, which is very helpful in composing.

However, for the most sophisticated user, even better synthesizers may be available in the future, based on systems such as the IBM PC, and offering a higher quality of sound because of the synthesizer components used. Packages already exist for more expensive computer systems, but these are beyond the price range we are considering.

If your child doesn't have a strong interest or lacks musical expertise, she can use a simpler product like the Commodore 64 with its built-in synthesizer, *if* a piano-like keyboard accessory becomes available for this computer.

Storage—A disk drive is needed for a sophisticated synthesizer, but otherwise is not essential. Again, check that the software package you are interested in is available on cassette, if you plan to use cassette storage.

Printer—A printer is not necessary unless your child is writing long programs with music commands and wants to list the program commands for easier checking and editing. A printer is also needed if you want to take advantage of software packages that print sheet music.

Memory—Producing or programming computer music doesn't require a lot of memory unless the software package or synthesizer your child is using requires it.

Suggestions—For live performance, at this time the upper end is an Apple IIe and an alphaSyntauri synthesizer; at the lower end, a Commodore 64. For composing or programming, a number of computers like the Acorn and Commodore 64 (both with particularly good music capabilities) or Atari may meet your child's needs.

Game Playing

Software—If your child's interest is in playing games on the computer, software is critical. If the games your child wants to play are not available on a computer, then the other aspects of the computer don't really matter. You and your child should look at some games on different computers to see which ones she likes best. Also go through some of the computer magazines to see what games your child is interested in and what computers they are available on. Once you know that there are games of interest to your child on a group of computers, you and she can evaluate the other features that make a game better or worse on a given computer.

Graphics—Even professional games-programmers are limited by the graphics available on a computer when they produce a video game. So if your child wants the effect of a true arcade game, you have to look for a computer system that produces those effects. In general, for games, you'll want higher resolution, more colors, and better animation. A younger child, however, may actually do better with a computer where the animation is not so rapid and may not need games that use the full capabilities of the computer's animation and graphics. Again, the best way to tell which computers have the right effects is to go to a computer store or two and look at some games on the systems you're considering.

Screen—Either a color TV or monitor are perfectly adequate for games. Width of text on the screen matters only if your child will be playing adventure games or others where she needs to be able to see a good deal of text on the screen at once; then 40 characters is preferable.

Joysticks—Joysticks or game paddles are crucial for most video games. If your child doesn't like the ones that come with the computer, you can probably buy joysticks that are more responsive from another manufacturer.

Storage—Games are available on cartridge, disk, and cassette, although not all computers can use all three forms of storage. Cartridge storage systems are probably best for game playing, because the cartridges are easier and faster to load than cassettes and don't require the extra expense of a disk drive or skill in using the disks. Cassettes are also acceptable forms of storage, but your child may tire of waiting for the largest of the games to load. Faster loading is available on high-speed cassettes. Going with a disk system just to play games doesn't make much sense, unless the games are very elaborate and are only available on disk or have significant educational value.

Memory—A large memory capacity is not needed for most games, especially those on cartridge. Check the memory requirements of the software you want to use to see if you are planning to get enough memory in your system.

Suggestions—Commodore 64 has nice games for children on cartridge. The Atari has many good arcade-style games. The Coleco Adam can play the wide range of game cartridge software that runs on the Colecovision game machine. There are a large number of games available on disk for the Apple IIe.

This is fine if you buy the Apple IIe for some other use and have the disk drive available. If not, the cost of the computer and disk drive makes the Apple IIe an expensive choice for game playing.

For a 10-year-old who wants to play games and for whom word processing is desirable to improve writing skills, we recommend the Coleco Adam for its game cartridges and built-in word-processing software. We also recommend the Atari.

Education

If your child will be using the computer for educational purposes, you have a list in Chapter 4 of the kinds of skills that should be covered in the programs she uses and the special characteristics she will need in these activities. As in game playing, the software you pick is crucial when it comes to education. You should look first for software that meets your child's needs. You'll probably find a software publisher whose materials you like and who will always tend to make that software available for the same group of computers. Or you may find that some computers have more educational software in general so you are more likely to find what your child needs with that computer. Once you've identified some possible computers, take other factors about them into account.

What you see—Color is good, but not essential. The number of characters displayed on a line can be critical because it determines the size of the type. For a younger child, you may well want larger type, 23 or 32 characters across instead of 40 or 64. Some computers offer two sizes of type on their 40-character or 64-character systems. The second size is double the size of the first, i.e., 20 or 32 characters across.

Graphics—Graphics can be helpful in getting educational points across and may even be crucial in some simulations. But you probably don't need the best graphics even in these cases. (On the other hand, too much graphic reinforcement can be distracting.)

Keyboard—The quality of the keyboard you should look for depends on the amount of typing required in the software your child will be using. If she will be *learning* typing from the computer, however, then a typewriter-quality keyboard is essential. You may want to pick a keyboard that is laid out like a standard electric-typewriter keyboard (with the apostrophe and semicolon in the middle row at the right rather than elsewhere on the keyboard) if you feel that your child should learn that kind of layout rather than the nonstandard layouts on some keyboards.

If your child is using the computer to learn business or finance-related subjects, she will probably want a keyboard that includes a numeric keypad on the side.

Function keys such as "HELP" keys are also increasingly important for educational uses. And if your child is learning from business or word-processing software, having "task keys" such as "PRINT," "SAVE," or "DELETE" can make learning easier.

Joysticks—These are used by some software, but are usually not required.

Synthesized speech—Speech can add a good deal to the value of educational software, giving spoken instruction to a child too young to read or pronouncing words in a reading, vocabulary or foreign-language course. Synthesizers are available as options on some computers. The software you use will have to be designed for use with the synthesizer. The Mockingboard synthesizer is used by some educational software.

Storage—As in games, cartridges are easiest for a child, especially a young child, to handle. However, more educational software is available on cassettes and disks, so you shouldn't limit your child to cartridge software. You may well have to invest in a disk drive to get the software you want.

Memory—As with games, the amount of memory you need is determined by the software you want to use. With disk-based software, however, you will need more memory just to use the disk drive. Also, as larger memory sizes become more common, more educational software developers will write software to take advantage of it.

Suggestions—Your choice of computer really depends on the software you pick. However, you should be aware that Apple has a great deal of educational software available; Atari also has much software, although probably not quite as much as

Apple. The Acorn computer has a great deal of software, developed in England, that is now becoming available here. The IBM PCjr is also attracting a great deal of educational software development.

For a family whose eight-year-old daughter needs help in math, we'd recommend considering one of the series of math games that cover math facts, logic, and word problems, available for the Atari. In addition, we'd recommend buying an inexpensive, third-party disk drive and 48K of memory, because these are required by the software. The girl could also play action games on cartridges with this equipment.

Other Activities

We haven't the room to cover all the possible activities your child might engage in, so you need to think about the kinds of features your child will need for any other activities you have in mind. Here are some guidelines to follow in determining which features your child needs.

First, if your child needs any special hardware, such as a special keyboard because of a disability, be sure that the computer you pick will accommodate that need. Check with the dealer or manufacturer of the special equipment to see with which computers it is compatible. If your child will be working with robots, hookups to a model railroad system, special printers, or any other special piece of equipment, you also need to be sure that she can use it with the computer you pick. Generally, the physical hookup to a computer is done through an interface like the RS–232 interface or through a board attachment to the computer, so you'll need to be sure that the appropriate port for that interface or the location for that board is available. Your child may also need software to allow control of the device, so be sure that is available as well.

Second, to determine what memory size you need, take into consideration the memory size required by any software your child will need. Activities involving the use of sophisticated programs like database management, financial calculation, or scientific applications will tend to require more memory, both for the software and for storing the work in progress. If your child's activity will require writing large programs, then she will need more memory for that as well.

In considering the type of screen and the text display, keep in mind that more sophisticated applications, like database work, are best done with an eighty-character display, which means your child needs a monitor. If your child will be looking at the screen for long periods of time, a monitor is a good choice to prevent eyestrain.

A printer is needed for any activity where your child wants a permanent record of the work done. It's also helpful for looking at a program and editing it.

If your child's activities will involve accessing databases like CompuServe or local bulletin boards, or involve sending messages to other computer users, then she will need a modem for communication. (Refer to Chapter 3 for a discussion of the types of modems and their relative advantages.) Some computers have built-in modems, other allow you to attach a modem directly to the computer through a port, still others require that you buy some kind of expansion box to use the modem.

COMPARING COMPUTERS

Information about the computer market is outdated as soon as it is written. The charts in Appendix B should give you a good head start in comparing computers and help you organize your research. You'll need to complete your research by consulting people at your computer store, ads in magazines, or computer buying guides with very recent information to find out what is true today about the computers you are interested in and what new computers have come on the market.

To use the charts in the appendix, look for the category that you are interested in on the chart headings (like Screen) and then read down the chart to see which computers have the kind of feature (like a 40-column display) that you want. Make note of the computers that have each feature. Continue to do this for each feature that you need. Look for the same features in other references. When you're done, you should find that one or more computers have most or all of the features you want. These are the computers that you'll choose among when making a final decision.

Price on the Charts

We have divided the computers in Appendix B into three price categories, and have presented information on computers in the same category together. The three categories are computers under $500, between $500 and $1000, and over $1000. You may well be able to find the computers discounted below these prices, and prices may have changed by the time you read this section, but the brands in each category should be roughly the same. You probably will want to look primarily at systems that are in your price range, and in the next range up as well.

The prices are list prices for the basic computer unit, that is, the minimum configuration offered by the manufacturer. *Figure B–1* shows what's included. In some cases, like the KayPro, for example, the manufacturer includes disk drives with the basic unit, so they are included in the price. Other manufacturers include different peripherals, like a printer or built-in modem, that are included in the price. The amount of memory is the minimum amount offered by the manufacturer.

CONSIDERING OTHER FACTORS

If you're lucky, you will find one perfect computer system that fits your child's needs and your pocketbook. On the other hand, you may find several that fit perfectly; you'll have to choose among them. Or you may have found several systems that each have features your child needs but not one that has all the features. In the narrowing-down process that you have to go through now, consider some other factors that may help you make your decision.

Who Else Will Use the Computer?

If you need a computer as well as your child, you might consider getting a computer that both of you can share. If you plan to use the computer for business or professional applications, this will probably mean getting one of the higher-priced systems that can handle word processing or spreadsheet work or whatever you need. You need to be sure that the system you pick will support the child's activities also. Otherwise, you might have to buy a separate system for yourself.

If your child is interested in graphics or in any of a wide range of activities that can be done on the IBM PC with the color board addition or on the Apple IIe, these might be good choices. These are general purpose machines, and a wide range of software is available for both you and your child. You might also consider one of the large number of IBM compatible machines (if they also have a color board), such as the Mindset or the Sanyo MBC-550. (You might also consider a low-end general purpose system such as the Sinclair QL.)

An increasing number of other business personal computers also offer high-quality color graphics that would be good for a child doing sophisticated-graphics programming. The Texas Instruments Professional Computer (which has an excellent keyboard layout) and the Sperry PC (from Sperry-Univac) exceed the IBM PC in high resolution and in range of colors. Both are IBM PC compatible and can also communicate with a wide range of mainframe computers. This would be useful for a parent who wants to tie in to a computer at work or for a student using a college computer system.

There are other good business machines. A well-engineered product that has very high resolution black-and-white graphics and is an excellent value is the Epson QX-10. The Epson QX-10 is very versatile and easy to learn to use, has a well designed keyboard, and includes very easy-to-learn word-processing software as part of the system. It would be a good choice for a child and a parent interested in word processing.

If your work is scientific in nature and your child is also interested in quite sophisticated mathematical or scientific applications, consider personal computer products from Hewlett-Packard and Digital Equipment Corporation (DEC). Hewlett-Packard personal computers, in particular, provide an extensive selection of mathematical and statistical analysis software. The HP-150 has a touch screen.

If you have several children, you will probably want to get a computer that meets all of their needs—unless one child will be going off to college and taking the computer along or unless there is a great difference in age or in potential computer activities. When you're buying for several children, you'll have to trade off between the kinds of activities that each child will be doing on the computer to be sure that all will be able to accomplish their primary goals.

Portability

If your child will be moving the computer around a lot, perhaps to a country house, a divorced parent's house, or a grandparent's house, you might want to consider a portable computer. These are designed to fold up so the computer keyboard, disk drives, and monitor make a compact package about the size of a small suitcase. (We are including in this category only the computers with full-screen displays, not the less versatile systems with only a few lines of text in view at one time.) IBM and Apple now have portable models.

If you can't get the features that your child needs in a portable, then consider getting a system that is easy to lift and move around. You may want to buy a carrying case that will hold all the components (except, usually, the monitor or TV).

What Computer Does Your Child Have at School?

If your child uses a computer at school, either for drill and practice or for programming, you should take this into consideration in selecting a home computer. There can be real advantages to having the same computer at home—but only, of course, if that computer meets your child's needs. If it does, then the fact that the same computer is available at school can tip the balance in favor of that computer for the home also.

It is often easier for a child to use a computer and software at home if she has learned how to use it in school. Turning on the computer, loading programs, and using the keyboard will all be familiar. For a young child or a child with a low tolerance for frustration, this can be very important.

If your school will lend software to your child to take home, then that's a reason to consider buying that type of computer. You might also want to buy the same software program your child is using at school so she can always use it at home too. Keep in mind that much school software is not available for, or not suitable for, home sale, so you may not be able to get the software.

If your child is learning programming at school and wants to work on programs at home, then there may be an advantage to having the same computer. Your child will be using exactly the same commands and working with exactly the same graphics at home as at school and can even bring home a disk or cassette to work on.

However, Logo languages and BASIC languages, especially those BASICs from the Microsoft company, are very similar on different computers, so it may not make much difference to your child that the languages she works on at home and school are different. In one family, one child was unwilling to make the effort to learn which commands were different at home, and therefore had trouble using her home computer. The other child in the family ran into the same situation, but was easily able to overcome the problem. The difference was probably one of personality. The second child had greater persistence and a more systematic way of approaching the problem.

If your child is programming graphics at school, it may be more important to have the same computer at home. Different BASICs handle graphics very differently. However, turtle graphics are very similar (and sometimes even identical) on different computers.

What Computers Do Friends Have?

This can be an important consideration. Children who have the same computer can trade software, write programs and run them on a friend's computer, and generally share in the culture of that computer. They can join, or form, a computer club. One group of children formed a software club, where each member of the group bought cartridges for the computer and then lent them out to the others in exchange for loans of their cartridges. Particularly for a child who is not terribly motivated to work with a computer, the incentive of having friends who are interested in that computer can be very helpful. For a shy child, the shared computer interest can be a way of making friends.

On the other hand, if the computer that a friend has does not meet your child's needs, it makes no sense to buy it. Even with different computers, the children can still send messages to each other via the phone lines or an electronic mail service, if they each have modems. Also, some computer clubs are built around interests rather than specific machines.

Future Needs

When you're considering what computer your child needs now, keep in mind that her needs may change in the near future. If your child is about to enter high school or college, you should consider buying a computer that will meet her needs then as well as now. (She'll probably want word processing, for example.) If your child has not been exposed much to computers yet, it's hard to predict in just what direction her interest in computers will grow. For example, don't assume that she won't want to program one because she expresses no interest in it now. Many children begin their computer experience by game-playing, but later become interested in programming either because they get bored with games, learn programming at school, or have a friend who introduces them to programming.

You may want to buy a slightly more expensive system than your child needs today, or a more flexible system that supports a broader range of activities, so that your child won't outgrow it too soon. Or you can buy an inexpensive computer now and plan to replace it with a better system once your child becomes more experienced and when new technologies become available and popular. The first computer can be discarded, sold, or given to a younger child in the family.

Weighing All the Factors

You and your child will have to weigh all the factors to come to a final decision. You will probably want to talk to computer-user friends and perhaps to teachers or resource people at your child's school. Visiting a computer show when there's one in your area can be an excellent way to see a number of computers and peripherals all at once, although you probably won't have the chance at a show to examine them very carefully. Finally, you should visit a few stores in your area to look at the systems you have in mind, see the software you would be buying, and talk to the computer salespeople there. The next chapter gives you some guidelines for talking to salespeople and testing computers in the store.

Once you and your child have actually looked over the systems you have in mind, you'll be in a position to decide which of the features found in the different systems are really important to you and to make your joint decision.

CHAPTER 6

Getting the Computer

Going to a store for the purpose of buying a computer intimidates some people. They feel helpless and out of place in a computer store. By now you have a good enough grounding in computers so that you shouldn't feel this way, but this chapter will give you some tips on talking to salespeople, getting the kind of assistance you need, and testing a computer to see if it meets your child's needs.

When you're ready to select a computer from the systems you've identified, you should see each computer in operation. You'll probably need to visit more than one store to see the systems you're considering, especially if one is a Radio Shack computer, because these are sold only at Radio Shack stores. It's important to go to the stores because it's impossible to tell from a list of specifications, pictures, or magazine reviews whether the computer is right for your child. For example, graphics which seemed not to have a high enough resolution may turn out to be perfectly fine once you see what can be done with them in a program. Music capabilities that looked good to you on paper may produce a sound you don't like. There's a good deal of personal taste involved in keyboard layout and feel, clarity of screen display, and appearance of color and graphics. You and your child really have to test these to make a decision.

CHECKLIST FOR A STORE VISIT

When you look at computers, bear in mind that you're trying to find out what the computer will be like for your child to use in your home. Your store may be running a great demonstration on the sound and graphics capabilities of a computer, but that's not much use to you when your child plans to do word processing on the computer. You should check on several things in the store:

> Is the computer easy enough for your child to use?
> Is the screen display adequate?
> Is the keyboard acceptable?
> Are special features—sound, color, graphics, animation—what you expected and what your child needs?
> Does the computer have the features you wanted and thought that it had—memory size, storage devices, etc.? Double check on your information.
> Does the software you plan to get meet your child's needs?

And you'll also want to know some things about the store:

> What is the store's price for this computer, and is it competitive with other stores?
> Are salespeople knowledgeable and helpful?
> What repair service is available for the computer and what are the conditions of service contracts?
> Is your child going to be able to visit the store by himself to buy additional hardware or software (assuming he's old enough and you want him to do this)? Some stores bar children unaccompanied by an adult.

Plan to visit the store with your child at least once. See a demonstration where both you and your child try out the computer and talk to a salesperson who knows that computer well. Look at software as well as hardware.

HOW TO TALK TO A COMPUTER SALESPERSON

Many people find it difficult to talk to salespeople in computer stores and are disappointed in the help they receive. This needn't be the case. Problems arise when customers try to get computer salespeople to help with the wrong things. For example, they try to get the salesperson to tell them which educational software to buy for their child when the salesperson doesn't know what areas the child needs help in and isn't an education expert anyway. You have the right to expect computer salespeople to have expertise in computers and peripherals and to be familiar with the software carried in the store. If they're experts in another field, like education, that's a plus, but don't expect it.

Instead, you should go to the store with a clear idea of the uses to which your child will put the computer and the features needed. Then you can ask the salesperson to show you these features on different computers and discuss these specific activities with you. You should know which software you need—at least the type of software and the features it should have. Perhaps you'll have titles in mind as well. The salesperson should then be able to help you pick out packages to look at from the store's stock. If you go to a computer store with this kind of approach, you'll help the salesperson focus on your needs and give you the best possible help.

Here are some tips to make your time with the salesperson more productive.

First, try to pick a time when the store is not terribly crowded. Saturdays tend to be busy; a weekday evening may be better. If you find the store is too crowded for the salespeople to spend much time with you, make an appointment to return at a better time.

When you meet a salesperson, tell him exactly what your child will be using the computer for, the features you think you need, and the computers you think would be suitable. Then get the salesperson's opinion on your choice. If he thinks you'll be happier with a feature on a different computer, have him show you the feature (for example, graphics) on both computers so you can compare. Even if he doesn't have a different recommendation, he'll be able to demonstrate the features you're interested in as he works with you.

Be sure to ask for explanations of any terms you don't understand. Also feel free to ask for clarification on any point. Computer salespeople don't always know your level of expertise and sometimes make statements that presume greater knowledge on your part than is really the case. When a salesperson makes a statement like "You need an RS-232C interface for that," ask any questions you need to get clarification. "Is that standard on this machine?" "How many separate items do I need to buy to get it?" "Can we accomplish the goal in another way without buying the interface?"

If you feel that your salesperson doesn't know enough about the computer or software you're considering, don't hesitate to ask if someone else in the store is the expert on that computer and if you can bring that person in on the discussion. If you can't get the help you feel is reasonable, go to another store.

You may feel that you shouldn't take up a lot of someone's time for a purchase of an inexpensive system. It's true that a computer store does not make much on the sale of each inexpensive computer, but remember that you'll be returning to this store for other purchases—software, peripherals, service, and maybe another computer someday. So you are a valuable customer, and you should feel free to ask questions.

Finally, ask the salesperson for a demonstration of the computer. The next section explains how to do this.

HOW TO WATCH (OR RUN) A COMPUTER DEMO

Trying out a computer is the key to answering most of the questions on our checklist. Often the store will have a computer demo program running continuously on one computer in the store. Typically this demo will show how the computer can be used in such different areas as education, games, and business. The demonstration may also exhibit some special features of the machine. This kind of demonstration will be entertaining and may show some features you're interested in. But to really try out the computer you will need to get a better demonstration from a salesperson or do one yourself with a salesperson's assistance.

There are two phases to a computer demonstration or tryout. In the first phase you and your child will try the keyboard, look at the display, and see how easy the computer is to set up and use. You'll need just one piece of software or none, but you will need the computer owner's manuals. In the second phase you'll look at the computer's color and graphics, listen to sound, check out the speed, and in general evaluate the special features and software your child needs. You'll need some software to help you put the computer through its paces. The first phase will take ten minutes or less; time for the second phase will vary depending on how many features you want to see and how much software you want to look at, but should take at least ten to fifteen minutes.

Explain to the salesperson that this is the kind of demonstration you have in mind. If she has time to go through the whole demonstration with you, helping you see and understand the computer features, that's ideal. But if she is too busy with other customers at the moment, then ask if she can help you pick out and load appropriate software as you need it and just leave you on your own in between.

To Begin the Demo

You will want to see the computer configuration or system you have in mind. If you are planning to buy a disk-drive system, then you'll want to see the computer running with a disk drive and see disk software. If you're planning to buy a cassette player, then that is what you want to see. You should see the computer with a color or monochrome (black and white, green, amber) display, depending on what you have in mind. Ask whether the screen for the store's computer is a TV or monitor. If the store uses a monitor and you're planning to use the computer with a color TV, bear in mind that the picture will not look as good on a TV. You should probably see the computer with a TV before you make your final purchase. It's less important that you see the computer hooked up to the printer you're considering; you can see the printer later with that or another computer.

First have the salesperson turn on the computer, showing you how to do it. You and your child should type something on the keyboard. Your objective is to feel the keyboard and see what the type looks like on the screen. Type the kinds of things you would type on a typewriter if you were trying it out. The quick brown fox is always useful here. Does the keyboard feel as you expected it to from your research? Is it adequate? How does the display look to you and, more important, to your child? Is it a readable typeface? Is it clear enough? You may have decided on 40 columns, but is this 40-column display readable for your child? Displays differ in the appearance of the letters, in their sharpness, and in background colors. You may decide at this point that with 40 columns of characters, the letters are too small for your young child to read. You may want fewer columns and larger type. Bear in mind that the size of the screen also affects the size of the image. If the TV is larger than the one your child will be using, the letters will be larger than they'll be at home.

Next, have the salesperson show you one software program from the stock for sale in the store. The first step in trying software will be to "load" the program. This means putting the disk in the drive or the cassette in the player or the cartridge in the machine, and getting the computer to transfer the program to its memory to start the program. (If you're really on your own in this demo, then read the instructions that come with the software and do it yourself. It's usually easy to do.) Watch the process and get the salesperson to explain each step. Keep in mind that your child will need to do this often. Is it easy enough for him? Have him try it too. (For a preschool child, this may not matter because you will probably be loading the software programs.)

The choice of software for the demo isn't terribly important, but you do want a program that will allow your child to respond to questions on the screen by typing an answer on the keyboard and that will show some text on the screen. Action games like Pac-Man won't serve the purpose.

Once the program has started, have your child read the screen, answer questions, type on the keyboard, etc. Judge the quality of the screen display and see if your child can find the necessary keys on the keyboard. While the main keys are always in the locations they are in on a typewriter, some keyboard layouts are less cluttered than others and some keys are labeled more clearly. This may be very important for a young child. Bear in mind that this is the first time your child has used the keyboard, and he will get better at it with practice.

Next, glance through the manuals that come with the computer. This is where you're going to turn for help in setting up the computer at home, learning to use it, and understanding what is happening when things go wrong. Is the manual clear to you? Can you understand how to set up the system? Will the instructions for using it be clear enough for your child if he is old enough to use the computer by himself? (A ten-year-old will be working alone a lot and trying to solve problems.) You've just seen how to load a program. Could you have understood the instructions in the manual?

If your child will be programming the computer, then investigate the language he'll be using. The salesperson or manual will tell you whether BASIC comes on a cartridge you have to plug in first or is automatically available when you turn on the machine. (Either method is fine.) If either you or your child knows some programming, then try out the BASIC on the computer. Make some errors in BASIC statements. How does the computer respond? Some computers highlight the place where you made an error. Some give helpful information on what you did wrong. Look at the error messages in the programming section of the manual. Is there such a list? Is the information given in a clear and helpful manner?

If your child knows BASIC, you should have him look through the list of commands in the manual to see how similar the BASIC on this machine is to the one he knows. The salesperson or the computer teacher at school may also be able to explain whether differences in BASICs are significant. As we said in Chapter 5, your child may have no trouble with slightly altered commands, or he may find them confusing.

If your child will be using other languages, he may also want to try these out. However, for languages like Logo and Pascal, where there may be rather large differences in the way the language is implemented on different computers, you and your child may want to read some reviews of the languages in computer magazines or talk to the salesperson or to the computer teacher at school. Sometimes, for example, you have a choice of different Logos for the same computer, put out by different companies. You will want to compare them for ease of use and for inclusion of features, such as sprites, that your child may want.

The Second Phase of the Demo

For this phase of the demonstration, you should see several pieces of software. You may have picked out some games or educational software that you want to try. Now is the time to try them. Or ask the salesperson which software will show the features you're looking for. Some possibilities would be a music utility, a graphics utility, a game with good graphics, word-processing software, etc.

Unless it is of no interest to you at all, see the graphics and/or sound capabilities of the computer. Do you like the look of the graphics and the quality of animation? You may need to see several software packages to judge the range available. Salespeople can be very helpful here; they have information on the capabilities of the computers they sell.

You'll probably see high-resolution graphics in the software you watch. If you're interested in low-resolution or character-set graphics because your child will be programming with them, look at these too. Ask the salesperson if there are any packages with these graphics. Not many software packages use these. You'll probably have to ask the salesperson to help you find the character-set keys on the keyboard so you and your child can try typing in graphics characters or to help the two of you try out low-resolution graphics.

Use a music software package or music demo program to listen to the computer's sound. Are the sound capabilities clear, rich, and easy to use? As we suggested in Chapter 5, you should read the manuals to see how difficult it is to program the graphics and sound and investigate any graphics utilities and music software that are available.

If your child will be using software for games, education, database work, word processing, etc., see some examples of the software available. Below, we discuss how to select a software package, but for now, look at the range of material available and see how your child reacts to the type of activity you have in mind. Let your child try out different software programs. Have the salesperson help you load them and explain how they work, if he is familiar with the packages. Otherwise look over the manual that comes with the software. You and your child won't be able to explore all the complexities of the software, but you should get a general feel for the program.

See whether the software does what you expected. Is the computer display adequate now that you're looking at the kind of software your child will be using? Is the speed of loading and saving programs, word-processed text, etc., fast enough? If not, it may be either because of the computer's limitations or because of limitations in the design of the software. Looking at some other software of the same type will help you judge where the problem is. If none of the software meets your child's needs, then the computer may not be adequate for your purposes.

If you intend to buy some extra hardware such as a printer, graphics tablet, lightpen, synthesizer, etc., you'll want to try these as well. Get a sample of the print from a printer. Try to see the tablet in operation with the computer. Try out the lightpen if possible. (Sometimes it's easier to do this kind of thing at a computer show where the manufacturers of these products display them, rather than at a computer store where the emphasis is on the sale of computers, not peripherals.)

This is a great deal for you and your child to absorb at once. If you're not ready to make a decision, go home and talk over what you've seen, read the literature you've gathered, and make a list of questions for the salesperson. Then, in a second visit, you can ask these questions and other questions about price, service, special interfaces for the peripherals you want, and other technical questions. If the answers are satisfactory, you'll be ready to buy on that second visit.

BUYING SOFTWARE

There's a good chance that software is so important to your child's computer activity that you can't buy a computer without it. Evaluating software will be an important part of the buying process. And once you've bought your computer, you'll probably find that your main concern will be software.

It's important that you try software before you buy it. At the very least, you should read the "documentation," the literature that comes with the software. Good documentation will show you sample screens that will give you an idea of how the program works.

How do you make a quick decision about whether the software you're considering is good and whether it suits your child's needs? Some of the criteria by which educators evaluate software can help you here. As you go over these criteria, keep in mind that software doesn't have to have a perfect score. You can judge which of these criteria mean the most to your child for a given activity. You can also decide to buy software that is weak in one area (for example, in the clarity of directions) if you can compensate for that (for example, by helping the child use it), especially if it has many other good features.

Here are some features that make it likely that your child will be able to use the software without problems.

> The software is easy to load, run, and use. It doesn't involve a lot of commands that are too difficult for your child.
>
> The printed instructions in the documentation are clear and your child can understand them.
>
> Directions on the screen are clear and unambiguous. When your child is supposed to respond to something, it's very clear which kind of response he should type (number, letter, word, special key, etc.).
>
> Once your child is familiar with the instructions, he can bypass them quickly.
>
> The readability level of the text on the screen is suitable for your child. To judge this, have your child try the software and read the text by himself.
>
> Your child can choose levels of difficulty, types of activities, and so forth, by himself, without your help.

If you're picking educational software, then besides being sure that the software is usable, you want to be sure that it will help your child learn. Here are some features to look for.

> The feedback in the program is immediate and helpful, telling your child that he's made an error and giving some kind of help in getting it right.
>
> The software doesn't let your child get caught in an endless circle of "Try again" if he can't answer a question, but eventually tells him the answer and moves on.
>
> The screen has a readable, uncluttered layout. Double spacing or large type may be helpful for young children.
>
> The type of response your child has to make is within his capabilities. For example, a young child who doesn't know the keyboard doesn't have to type long answers; if a joystick is used, your child can control it easily.
>
> Your child can revise his answers by backspacing if he makes a typing error or changes his mind. The computer should

usually respond only when he types RETURN to show his answer is complete.

The speed of presentation of text is controlled by your child. He won't miss information because the computer clears it from the screen before he can read it. The computer should proceed only when he indicates he's ready (usually by pressing the spacebar or RETURN).

The tone of address is friendly, not insulting to the student if he makes an error.

The type of graphics and motif of the software is acceptable to you. If you don't like your children to watch violence on TV, you may not want shooting in an educational game either.

The software doesn't put lectures or long written passages on the screen. That kind of information is better conveyed by a printed textbook.

Help is available within the program if your child gets stuck.

Graphics, sound, and color are integrated into the activity, not just an afterthought.

The software uses the conventions your child is familiar with. For example, in an addition problem, you child adds the ones column and then the tens, and so on, working from right to left; in a phonics program, the phonetic symbols are familiar.

WHERE TO BUY THE COMPUTER

When it comes to actually buying a computer, your choices are a computer store, a department store, a discount store, a mail-order house, and a computer show. The principal differences will be in price, service, and availability of help, before and after you buy.

You should expect to get the most help from salespeople in a computer store and far less help from a discount or department store—unless it has a real computer store within it. The salespeople in a discount or department store may have no training in computers at all. Mail-order houses differ in the amount of help they offer. Some will simply ship the product to you; others will talk to you about your purchase and offer help over the phone afterwards. They can't offer the personalized help of a good computer store, however.

Prices in discount stores and mail-order houses tend to be

lower than computer store prices, although there is quite a variation in price in computer stores as well. Some computer stores advertise that they are the lowest in price, and they can meet a discount store's price. They will probably give less help, however. Department stores vary in price, but are generally higher than discount stores.

When you buy via mail-order, you can usually get service from the mail-order house, but you'll have to mail the computer or peripheral back. Discount houses and department stores will also, typically, mail the computer to another location for service. You may have the option, instead, of taking it to an authorized service center at a local computer store. Computer stores usually have their own service shops on the premises and give the fastest turn-around time.

The decision on where to buy involves a trade-off between price on the one hand and help and service on the other. You can see that a computer store will offer more of the latter but possibly at a higher price.

Our recommendation is that, especially for an inexpensive or moderately priced computer, you buy at a computer store and not worry about the rather small dollar-amount you could save by going elsewhere. Assuming that you do find the store helpful and that service is available there, you'll probably be happiest with this choice. You will have salespeople available to answer at least some of your questions after you buy, and you will establish a relationship that makes it easier to get information on peripherals and software. As novice computer users, you and your child will need support.

If you're buying a more expensive computer, then the discount from a mail-order or discount house will save you more money. You have to decide whether the support or the money is more important to you. If you can get support from a friend who owns that computer or from a computer club, or if your child is very knowledgeable, then you may decide that you don't need all the help the store offers. On the other hand, if the salespeople at the store have been very helpful to you, doing the kind of demonstration we outlined in this chapter and answering your questions, then you may feel a certain obligation to buy there.

Obviously, if you find the store is not helpful to you, if the people don't seem knowledgeable, and if they don't appear to offer support to their customers, then there is no point in buying at the store at all.

A computer show is another possible place to buy. Usually most of the vendors at the show will be local computer stores. They will be offering "show specials," which is one way to get a discount price from a dealer. Other vendors will be peripheral manufacturers and mail-order houses, and you can get discounts from them at a show as well. You will also have a chance to get more information on peripherals from the manufacturers than your local store can often provide.

Once you've purchased a computer and are looking for peripherals, we recommend considering sources other than a computer store. The exception is buying a printer for use with a word-processing package. Many people have some difficulty getting a word processor to communicate correctly with a printer. The reason for this is that each word-processing package must be equipped to send signals to all the many printers on the market. The person who uses the package must give it some specific information on what kind of signal his printer needs. (Information might include type size, space between lines, how underlining is done, where line feeds are needed, etc.) If you buy computer, software, and printer from one store, where a salesperson is familiar with the system and possible trouble spots, you'll assure that your child will receive the help he needs to get things set up quickly. Even if you pay a little more for the printer, you'll gain in the long run.

For purchasing a printer for other uses and for purchasing other peripherals, you could consider saving money with a discount house or mail-order house. You probably won't get as much help in these purchases from your store as you did when you bought your computer anyway. Salespeople can't be knowledgeable about all the different peripherals on the market. Service is often done by the manufacturer rather than the store. Check into this for each peripheral. On the other hand, especially if the dollar difference is small, it can be very convenient to buy from your local store.

When it comes to software, if your local store lets you preview software, that can be a very strong argument in favor of buying at the store. Mail-order houses often let you return the software if you don't feel it's right for your child, after you've examined the documentation, but they usually won't accept returns on software once the disk or cassette package has been opened. Stores that specialize in software are opening up all over the country, and these may be the best places to buy software. They will almost always let you preview in the store, and some will let you take the software home, try it out, and return it if you don't like it.

By the way, if you have questions on software that neither the documentation nor your dealer can answer, you can often call the publisher of the software and ask questions, sometimes on a toll-free number. Especially for more expensive software, like word-processing software or CP/M-based software, the publishers will have technicians available to help you with your problems.

Once you've bought your computer and brought it home, you'll have the exciting task of helping your child to get the most from this new purchase. The next chapter will help you to do this.

CHAPTER 7

After You Buy

HOW TO BEGIN

Bringing home a new computer for your child is the start of an adventure. You'll naturally have high hopes for the benefits your child will gain from the computer. This chapter will give you some suggestions to help your child get the most from the computer.

It's important at this point to remember that the computer is not a substitute for all the other educational, creative, and fun things in your child's life. Although it's tempting to place all the emphasis on this piece of technology, a computer is only one of the many tools your child needs to grow. Books, games, toys, crayons, and the like are still essential to your child's growth. A computer will enrich your child's life and add to the total of all the good experiences you provide for her.

INTRODUCING YOUR CHILD TO A COMPUTER

The computer that you've bought belongs to your child and you want her to get the most from that computer. This means that you have to give your child a real measure of control over how the computer is used, just as you give her control over the use of a Lego set, stamp collection, train set, dollhouse, etc. If your child is free to use the computer in a way that seems reasonable to her, she'll appreciate it and grow with it. Your role is to guide your child, offering help when necessary and monitoring what's going on as you do with other activities. For example, you'll decide where the computer will be placed, how two children will share it, and how many hours the computer can be used if it starts to interfere with other activities. If you have a very young child, you'll have a greater role to play in helping with activities, especially in the early stages.

The first step for you and your child will be to unpack the computer. It's a good idea to unpack the computer manual first, and follow the step-by-step instructions given there on unpacking and connecting the various computer parts. First, it's good for your child to learn that the answers to questions about the computer will be in that book. Second, you'll both have a much easier time if you read the instructions instead of trusting to instinct. Don't worry though; setting up a computer is usually not very complicated. If your child has the same computer at school, she may be able to do much of the setup by herself. You don't need to pick a permanent location for the computer now. Set it up in the living room or wherever is convenient.

It's a good idea for you and your child to pick something rather simple and short with which to start. When the computer is very new, the excitement of having it in the house may make it difficult to concentrate on more complex computer activities. When you buy a computer and the software that you know your child will need, be sure to include one easy-to-use piece of software, like an action or educational game, to have something to use to become familiar with the computer at home. Instead of having your child start to learn the word-processing package that she'll be using, suggest that she play the game.

If your child will be doing programming and has learned some programming at school on this computer, then she may want to try out a simple program first. But if she hasn't used this computer before or isn't a very good programmer, again, it may be better to start with a game.

Once your child has had a chance to try out the computer by using the game, you'll want her to begin using the computer for other activities. Bearing in mind that you bought a computer to further your child's interest in a number of areas, to help with some academic areas, and perhaps to further a career interest, it should be easy to guide your child to another activity. As we said earlier, you'll want to encourage her to pick an area of high interest first, not an academic area where she is having difficulties. If you've followed the plan in this book, you'll have the proper software so she can begin this activity quickly.

Your role, at this point, is to help your child to get into the activity quickly and easily. This may mean helping her to read instructions, load a program, and begin to use it. It may mean loading the program for a young child and sitting with her as she uses it for the first few sessions. It may mean simply listening to your child when she describes the kinds of programs she plans to write.

WHAT HAPPENS NEXT

After the first few weeks, it's quite possible that your child's interest in the computer will slacken a bit. This is a typical pattern as the newness of the computer wears off. After working on the computer every day after school for the first few weeks, one boy now works in fits and starts. When he has a new game or a new idea for a program, he uses the computer furiously for a few days. Then he may not touch it again for a week or more. Similarly, one ten-year-old girl, using her parents' elaborate music-synthesizer computer system for songwriting, will not use the system for several weeks at a time, but then will get an inspiration and write as many as twenty-five melodies in a single evening. If you've identified areas that are of interest to your child and you provide the necessary software, you'll find your child will not abandon the computer completely.

You may also find that your child moves from project to project on the computer, perhaps not even finishing the projects. Several parents have found that their children will use the computer for a project each time a new interest emerges in their lives. One boy began to put all of the statistics for all the baseball players in the American League in a database. The job was too large for him, so he stopped after getting his favorite team done. Then he used the computer as a tutor for his Spanish class, writing a program that gives him Spanish words and asks him for the English translation. Then he abandoned this project and used the computer to do calculations for a science experiment. Each time he worked on a project, he learned more about the computer and also more about the subject he was working on. Even though many of the projects proved too large for him to handle, he learned a great deal from each one.

On the other hand, some children complete a computer project and adapt it as a regular work tool. Another boy also wrote a Spanish–English word-quiz program when he was studying elementary Spanish. He still uses the program now that he is taking advanced Spanish in school.

A computer project can be a stimulus for the child to extend computer and problem-solving skills in new directions as interests change—as happened with the first boy. Or it can be an opportunity to create useful permanent tools that help further each interest—as happened with the second boy.

You can help your child use the computer effectively by keeping an eye on what she's doing and occasionally suggesting ways that the computer could be a tool for a school project or an interest she's pursuing. Keep in mind the ways you thought your child would want to use the computer and help to pursue these by providing software or suggestions. Remember also that your child is growing and new areas of possible computer activity will emerge all the time. For example, one family bought a computer for their child to do programming because he was learning programming in school. The next year, when he was assigned a research paper as a project at school, they bought a word-processor software package for him to use for that paper and subsequent papers.

You may even want to do a project together in an area of mutual interest. You and your child may want to learn how to use a word processor, database system, or financial planning tool. You would be learning it to help you in your work or home interests while your child would learn it to help with schoolwork or hobbies. Or, if you share an interest like genealogy, travel, or music with your child, you might want to use the computer to pursue that interest together. Your whole family may occasionally want to play some computer games or puzzles together, just as you would play a board game or a word game. You can go a step further and design your own game. For example, if you all enjoy word games, you might design and program a simple word game, taking advantage of the computer's storage and display capabilities.

OVERCOMING PROBLEMS

Some problems are bound to arise over such issues as how much time your child should spend with the computer, how two children can share the computer, etc. This section will give you some strategies for handling or avoiding problems.

When Your Child Spends Too Much Time on the Computer

Although you want your child to use the computer and get all possible benefits from it, you certainly don't want her to neglect her schoolwork. Many parents have found that their child spends so much time on computer projects that homework goes undone. Their child disappears into her room after school, after dinner, and at any other opportunity and works on the computer. While you certainly don't want to discourage interest in the computer, you can set up rules as many other parents have. One mother says that once or twice a year she finds her son is spending too much time on the computer. She can tell when the time arrives because his homework doesn't get done. At those times she puts her computer rules into effect. She has found that if she insists that homework be done first, her son will do a slapdash job on his assignments so as to get to the computer. So her solution is to restrict the number of hours a day and the times of the day when her son can work on the computer. This insures that he has time to do his homework and time to spend with the family.

Many parents also worry that children who spend all their free time at the computer will become loners, with no friends. In general, having and using a computer doesn't change a child's social relationships much at all. A child who spent time alone reading or doing other activities before may continue to spend time alone with a computer, but a gregarious child will not neglect friends and other activities. The effects of the computer tend, if anything, to be beneficial. Computers have given many shy children an opportunity to make new friends among the other computer users in their class with whom they have interests in common. If you feel that your child is not socializing as much as before, you might suggest that she join a computer club at school or invite a friend over to play games on the computer.

When Two Children Share a Computer

If you have bought a computer for two or more children to share, you'll find yourself witnessing or refereeing disagreements on whose turn it is to use the computer. Typically, one child gets possession of the machine and won't give it up to the other. To remedy this situation, you might try the solution arrived at by schools where one computer has to be shared by many children. Some schools place time limits on the length of time each child can use a computer. Many have a sign-up system so that children can sign up for half-hour or one-hour blocks of time. Children are restricted from signing up for consecutive blocks of time or for repeatedly signing up for the most popular times. When the time is up, it's the child's responsibility to stop what she's doing and find the next user. You might find that a sign-up system works even if you have only two children, particularly if they both want the computer right after dinner and can't agree on any less formal way of assigning use.

If you have two children who are doing programming on the computer, you will find a printer a good investment. When a child cannot get to the computer, she can work at her desk on the printout of her program, adding lines and looking for program "bugs." This is a good programming technique. You can also enforce the rule many schools have, that programs have to be written first on paper (also a good programming practice) and then entered and tested on the computer.

When the Computer Disturbs Someone Else

If your child has ever had a video game, talking teaching machine, or other noisy toy, you know how annoying the noise can be to adults. Many computer activities, especially video games and educational games, will also be noisy and irritating if the computer is in the same room with you. You may also find that when you want to watch television, your child has the computer hooked up to the TV. The solution to the second problem is obvious; buy a monitor or TV with the computer. If the noise becomes a problem, you'll have to reconsider the placement of the computer.

Many people like to have the computer in a place where everyone in the family can use it, but if that disturbs you or if conversations disturb the child working at the computer, then move the computer to the child's room. If two children share the computer, then it may have to be moved periodically or one child may have to agree to let the other use it in her room.

Eyestrain and Other Hazards

There has been a great deal of publicity about the hazards of video display terminals and computers on the job. People who use these for many hours a day complain of eyestrain, fatigue, and muscular strain in the neck and arms. There is some concern about the low levels of radiation emitted by the computer monitors as well. Although it's unlikely that your child will be using the computer for such long stretches of time, you may still want to protect her from any possible hazards by taking these precautions:

Place the computer in a location where the area around the computer will be well lit so that books and papers are readable. Be sure that the light does not fall directly on the computer screen, because this causes reflection and makes the screen hard to read.

Look at the room at the times of day when your child will be using the computer. Where does the light from the windows fall in the room? Don't place the screen on that wall.

To prevent neckstrain that results from holding the head in an awkward position while looking at the screen, the computer should be set up so that the screen is at your child's eye level. This almost always means that you have to elevate the screen on a stand or box.

Especially if your child is using the computer for word processing or using the keyboard for a lot of typing, the keyboard should be at typewriter height so she doesn't have to raise her arms too high to type. Typewriter height is approximately 26 inches for an adult, lower than desk height. If you don't have a choice of height for the computer table, then consider altering the height of the chair, perhaps by putting a cushion on it. It might also be worthwhile to consider a chair with adjustable height. These are sold in art-supply stores as chairs for graphic artists and at office-furniture stores. Also be sure the chair has good back support.

It's unlikely that there is any real danger from radiation when your child is using a computer screen. However, just to be safe, don't let your child use a color monitor or color TV that is just a few inches in front of her face. Keep the set a comfortable viewing distance from your child. This will reduce eyestrain as well.

Guarding Against Equipment Damage

Computers are not especially delicate pieces of equipment, but they do need some sensible care. Follow the instructions for care and maintenance in your computer owner's manual. In addition, you may want to establish some rules for safe use of the computer. For example, you should probably not allow your child to eat or drink at the computer. Spilling soft drinks into the computer is one sure way to damage it.

You should also be sure your child keeps cassettes, cartridges, and diskettes in a dust-free location. A cassette should be kept in a plastic cassette case. Special cautions that should be taken with diskettes are often listed on the diskette label. Be sure that your children don't bend the diskettes or leave them in a cold or hot spot (like a radiator or in the sun on a windowsill).

If your child must move the computer or connect new pieces of equipment to it, you should be sure, first of all, that she is old enough to handle the electric plugs safely. Have her turn the computer off before connecting or disconnecting anything. Again, your computer manual is your best source of information on this.

Static electricity can cause real problems (temporary) with a computer. If the computer is in a carpeted room where static charges build up easily, you might need an antistatic mat, available at office supply stores, under the chair. If you're planning to carpet the room, buy antistatic carpet.

When Your Child Has a Modem

Problems can arise when your child has a modem connected to a phone line and to the computer. The newspapers are full of stories about children who "break into" computer data banks using their home computers and a modem. It does not seem to require any extraordinary degree of computer skill to do so. The children who break into data banks do so just for the fun and challenge of it, and most don't realize that they can cause damage or that they may be committing crimes. It's a parent's responsibility, therefore, to make sure that children *do* understand that such actions can cause havoc.

While it's highly unlikely that your child would ever attempt to break into a database, you should discuss the subject with your child and be sure that she understands the possible consequences of what seems like an innocent trick. Explain that once you have access to a private information bank whose workings you're not familiar with, it's easy to accidentally alter a file or erase vital information. The boys who broke into the patient information file at Memorial-Sloan Kettering Hospital, for example, could have accidentally damaged files of information on cancer patients in treatment at the hospital. When an intrusion is discovered, it can take hours or even days for workers to restore the information or make sure damage has not occurred. You can explain that part of growing up and becoming an adult involves developing appreciation and respect for the privacy of other people, including both data about them and data that belongs to them.

HELPING YOUR CHILD USE THE COMPUTER

Some parents feel a bit overwhelmed when their child begins programming the computer or doing other projects with it. In other activities that their child undertakes, the parents are familiar with the tasks and can offer constructive help. But many parents feel they don't know enough about computers to be of help to their children. However, without knowing any programming, it is possible to give your child some guidance when she's involved in a computer project.

You can be of most assistance to your child when she is planning a project. Keep two things in mind.

First, the project should be of manageable size for your child. If you find that your child is planning what seems to you a very large project, offer some guidance to cut it down to size. If, for example, your child is planning to put information on a large number of books into a database so you'll have a record of what you have and where it is, you could suggest that she start with just her own books and then add the rest of the family books when that's accomplished. This will help make the job simpler and will help insure that she gets a sense of accomplishment from it even if she only does the first task. If your child is planning to use a new word-processing package, you might suggest that she start by typing just a few sentences to try out the commands for saving and printing, then try out editing commands and other features one at a time. Many word-processing packages come with a series of lessons on how to use the program. Working through the lessons would also help your child learn the system a piece at a time.

If your child is writing her own programs, it may be especially necessary to help her to keep the task a manageable one. The best guidance you can give (and what the best professional programmers do) is to divide the program she plans to write into several smaller subprograms. Then she can write each subprogram and make sure it works before going on to the others. If she is planning, for example, to write a program to give a multiple-choice test using the computer (a common idea among children), then she should break the task down into subtasks: The computer has to get the questions from storage in the program, print questions on the screen, check answers, and keep score. Each of these can be a separate "module" of the program. It can be written and debugged before going on to the other modules. It isn't really necessary for *you* to break down the program into modules, but you can listen to your child discuss the task and help her to figure out the best approach herself.

The second kind of guidance you can offer your child involves being sure she has the necessary tools to do the project.

One kind of tool is the child's own knowledge of programming. If your child is planning, for example, to write a video-game program, and she is a novice programmer, she probably doesn't have the skills to do it. You might suggest instead that she copy some game programs from computer magazines and then try modifying them. Or you might suggest that she write a word game, a number-guess game, or something that doesn't involve complex graphics. Doing these tasks will help her improve programming skills and prepare for the larger task.

Your child may also need special hardware or software tools to do her project. As we discussed in Chapters 4 and 5, there are a number of software programs or special tools, like graphics tablets, that can make graphics and music much easier to do. Your child may be planning to write a program to do something like database work when she could buy a program to let her do this instead. The two of you have to decide whether her goal is to use the database, in which case she should buy a commercial program, or to learn how to write that kind of program herself. Even when a child is programming, there may be tools that will help with the task. A number of "programming utilities" are available. These help with tasks like combining two programs, renumbering programs, and tracing program logic to aid in debugging. If you and your child make an occasional trip to the computer store to see what's available and read computer magazines, you'll become aware of tools that can help in these areas.

HOW TO PICK A COMPUTER SCHOOL OR CAMP

The *New York Times Magazine* has a section of advertisements for summer camps. Virtually every one of the dozens of camps advertised there now claims to offer computer instruction. The situation is the same in other areas of the country. Traditional camps offer programming as an activity, and there are computer camps, computer day camps, and computer schools. If you decide that your child would enjoy and benefit from computer camp or instruction at a computer school, how do you pick one?

The first thing you'll want to find out is how much access your child will have to a computer. How many computers are there and how many students? There should be at least one computer for every two students in a class. Students should have access to the computers after class or in free time, as well, to practice and do homework assignments.

In addition to access to computers, your child needs access to instructors for special help. Most learning of programming takes place not in formal classes but in lab sessions when each student works on individual programming assignments. How many students are assigned to each teacher? There's no hard-and-fast rule on teacher–student ratios, but smaller class sizes will make it more likely that your child will get enough help. Find out whether there will be teachers available in lab sessions or after class.

The quality of the instructors makes a big difference in the quality of the class. Ideally, you want teachers who have both teaching and programming experience. Programming teachers from local schools who work at the camp or at the computer school after regular school hours will probably do the best job. Teachers who have learned programming themselves may also be good. Professional programmers or amateur programmers—for example, parents who have learned programming—who have no teacher training or other teaching experience can also be good, but you'll want to judge how well they present material to students. Talking to students who have taken classes at the school and to their parents will help you decide. At the bottom of the scale are people whose only qualification is that they have been trained by the school to be programming teachers. It's unlikely that they will have the breadth of experience necessary to do a good job.

The type of computer and the language taught is also a concern. The language should be the same as the child will be using at home. If the child uses Logo, then he should go to a camp that teaches Logo.

You'll also want to know how the curriculum and learning materials were developed. It's probably best when the curriculum is established by the school rather than developed by each teacher, particularly when the teachers are not professional teachers of programming. You'll know that each student will be exposed to this core of knowledge and that appropriate materials will be available to support the instruction.

In the case of a computer camp setting, it can also be helpful if the computer activity is integrated in some way with other special interests such as music, art, science, or foreign language learning. The result can be a much richer and more motivating experience that makes a lasting impression on the child.

When you're thinking of computer school or camp for your child, don't forget that your child can also learn or improve her programming skills on her own with the help of books and computer magazines. A number of magazines run series of programming lessons and often have articles on programming as well. See Appendix A for a list of popular magazines. There are also books on programming designed especially for children, as well as a large number of books for a general audience.

HOW WILL A COMPUTER AFFECT YOUR FAMILY?

Having a computer-literate child can make some subtle and some not-so-subtle changes in your family. Parents whose children are proficient with computers sometimes say that they feel their children talk a new language that they, the parents, can't understand. Many parents are very impressed by their children's accomplishments and feel a new respect for their children. Both of these feelings are very natural when children acquire skills that are highly valued in society today. In a way, the children have stepped into the adult world, and this is bound to have some effect on their relationship with their parents.

The clearest case of a change in relationship occurs in those cases where a child begins to use her programming skills to earn money. Some of these children, who sell computer games to publishers or get parttime jobs in a local business, may earn substantial amounts of money. One teenage boy actually made more money than his parents. When your child is not dependent on you financially any more, although she still needs your guidance and help in other ways, you have to be ready to handle a very new, untraditional relationship.

This kind of extreme change in the parent-child relationship is very rare, but other parents also report that the balance has changed a little because of their child's new knowledge. One mother even said that she wouldn't show any interest in computers to her ten-year-old son because she knew that he would want to teach her about the computer, and she is used to being the one to do the teaching. She realized that she couldn't handle this switch in roles. It would be better if she could accept that her child knows more in this one area and try to share his excitement with him.

Try having your child show you some of what she's learning and doing. If she's not a very good teacher—and a lot of children aren't—then don't have her try to teach you programming. Just ask her to show you how she accomplished a particular task.

You might also ask your child to do some programming for you. Many parents report that their children are very eager to write a program for them. Your child might do a program for you to compute your gas mileage, manage a budget, or keep track of ticket sales for a charity event. You can work with your child to decide what the program should do, what any printed reports should look like, and what the logic of the program should be. Even though you don't know programming, you do understand more than your child about the subject involved. You know how to compute gas mileage on paper, for example, or what categories to include in a budget.

If you are really interested in computers, you might want to take a course along with your child or join a computer club together. One group of California parents found a way to keep up with their computer-literate children and benefit the school as well. They arranged for the school's parent association to offer a course in BASIC programming for parents, to be taught by a college computer teacher. Some parents who have completed the course now work in the elementary school's computer lab during the day as aides, helping young children with their programming projects and guiding the children in how to help each other.

Whichever way you choose to respond to your child's growing knowledge about computers, you can find it a positive influence on your lives, giving you a new area to share.

One very positive benefit of a computer in a family can be the effect it has on the relationship between several children in the family. As we have said, children working with computers tend to show more cooperative behavior. This can be true in a family as well. One thirteen-year-old boy takes the time to load programs for his four-year-old sister and to show her how to use them. Another teenage girl who has learned programming helps her younger brother who is just starting a programming course at school. Frequently, when two children in the family know programming, they help each other over rough spots and help debug each other's programs. There are very few other areas in which children are as interested in helping each other.

SUPPORT FOR YOUR CHILD

Your child will need support and stimulation to continue to grow with the computer. Joining a computer club, taking a computer course at school, subscribing to a computer magazine, or reading a book on computers can all help provide that support. (When grandparents ask what they can give your child for a birthday present, you might suggest a subscription or computer book.) Check in magazines for national and regional computer clubs (also called users' groups) that have meetings in your area. Also check for clubs at school and elsewhere in the community. Your local computer dealer or the computer teacher at school may know of some, and others can be found on computer electronic bulletin boards.

Remember also that individuals as well as institutions can play a very important role in stimulating and supporting your child. Individuals such as your child's friends, older cousins, friends of the family, and teachers at school may all influence and inspire your child at various times to become involved in a new stage of computer activity. They may demonstrate uses of the computer that are new to your child or act as computer-using role models.

One child went through four distinct stages of influence over about a four-year period. He was first exposed to computers as a learning tool at school, then he became interested in playing computer games through a friend, later he developed an interest in programming through an older cousin, and finally decided, on his own, to go to a computer camp to learn advanced programming techniques. Each stage propelled the child to a higher level of computer awareness and sophistication.

YOUR CHILD'S GROWTH AND
THE COMPUTER'S EVOLUTION

A child will have very different views of the computer and how to use it at ages five, eight, twelve, and fifteen. Her perception of the possibilities inherent in the computer will change as her world-view changes. Tools take on different meanings as the child's cognitive abilities grow and the child's interests shift and mature. In particular, the significance of the computer as a writing tool, categorizing tool, planning and analyzing tool, and artistic tool will increase for the child as she develops intellectual and esthetic skills. You should take this into account when you think about how your child will be using the computer in the future, and allow for growth.

At the same time, keep in mind that the microcomputer field itself will not be standing still. In the past, about every three years the personal computer as a product has gone through a major change, reflecting both new technological developments, new marketing initiatives, and consumer readiness. The personal computer itself and what people have expected of it have been very different in 1975, 1978, 1981, and today. Such changes do not come about at one time, but their cumulative effect and consolidation over a three-year period leads to a qualitatively new stage in the development of the personal computer as a market product. In turn, new capabilities in hardware products make possible significant new developments in software, which in turn can support new kinds of interests.

This trend will continue in the future. For example, by 1987 there will be major changes in the music capabilities of home computers because of increases in memory size and speed of processing. By 1990 there will be major developments in video processing and animation because of optical disk storage. By 1993 the so-called fifth generation ("artificial intelligence") computers should be influencing home computer technology. These products will have a greater ability to understand natural language, which will change the nature of programming and information gathering with the computer.

Be prepared every few years, as your child grows, to deal with the qualitative changes in your child and in the kinds of computers and software that are available. You'll want to use the techniques in this book to analyze your child's needs at that time and to see what computer activities and computer tools will meet those needs.

In buying a computer for your child, you become part of a changing world in which the small, powerful microcomputer will become a tool for use by everyone, young and old. As your child grows up and enters the adult world, computers will be part of many aspects of her life. You need to provide your children with experiences that will help them to cope with this new world and to take advantage of the many opportunities it holds. Buying a computer for your child and helping your child use that computer are steps you can take to help her grow and thrive in this new and challenging world.

Computer Magazines

Following is a list of magazines that you and your child might find helpful in your search for a computer and software, and as you work with the computer. Note that some of the magazines actually come on diskettes to be used with your computer.

Most of these magazines are available in computer stores and on some newsstands. If they aren't available in your area, you can write for information.

Magazines for Parent and Child

BYTE
70 Main Street
Peterborough, NH 03458

A very technical magazine. Best for the advanced computer user.

Compute!
515 Abbott Drive
Broomall, PA 19008

Especially useful for the actual programs it contains for many of the major computers. Many children enjoy typing these programs into their computers and then running the programs.

Creative Computing
P.O. Box 789-M
Morristown, NJ 07960

A general computer magazine, including hardware and software reviews. Some articles of interest to the beginner and to the more experienced user.

Family Computing
Scholastic, Inc.
1290 Wall Street West
Lyndhurst, NJ 07071

Primarily for the novice. Oriented toward children and family use of computers.

PC Magazine
Ziff-Davis Publishing Company
One Park Ave.
New York, NY 10016

For users of IBM PC and the IBM compatibles. Contains hardware and software reviews and articles primarily of interest to IBM users.

PCjr Magazine
Ziff-Davis Publishing Company
One Park Ave.
New York, NY 10016

For users of the IBM PCjr. Hardware and software reviews and articles on using the PCjr.

PC World
555 De Haro St.
San Francisco, CA 94107

For users of IBM PC and compatible computers. Contains hardware and software reviews and articles on using the IBM PC.

Personal Computing
P.O. Box 1408
Riverton, NJ 08077

Nontechnical, home and business orientation. Contains hardware and software reviews.

Popular Computing
70 Main Street
Peterborough, NH 03458

Nontechnical magazine for home and business users, oriented toward the beginner. Contains hardware and software reviews.

Portable Computer
500 Howard Street
San Francisco, CA 94105

For users of the more than 100 types of portable computers, including KayPro and Compaq. Hardware and software reviews and comparison charts plus articles on portable computers.

Softalk
Box 60
North Hollywood, CA 91603

For users of Apple computers. Contains articles for beginners and advanced users, software and accessory reviews. Apple owners can get one free trial subscription by sending name, address, and Apple serial number to magazine.

Magazines for Children

Digit Magazine
P.O. Box 29996
San Francisco, CA 94129

Articles for children on computer use, programming, children who use computers. Contains activities for children to do with or without a computer. Reviews by children.

Enter Magazine
Children's Television Workshop
One Lincoln Plaza
New York, NY 10023

Articles for children on computers and video games. Reviews of software and games by children. Activities to teach programming with and without a computer.

K Power
Scholastic, Inc.
1290 Wall Street West
Lyndhurst, NJ 07071

Articles of special interest to teens and preteens on computers.

Disk Magazines

Microzine
Scholastic, Inc.
1290 Wall Street West
Lyndhurst, NJ 07071

Available for several different computers, including Apple, Franklin Ace, and Atari. Games, stories, and interviews all presented via the computer screen.

Window
469 Pleasant St.
Watertown, MA 02172

Available for Apple and other computers. Articles, features, reviews presented via the screen. Software reviews contain excerpts from the programs. Includes games, educational games, instructional programs, and useful utilities like a music composition program.

Computer Information Charts
FIGURE B–1 / **Basic Configuration**

	A. LOW-PRICED
	Basic System (Shows items included in the base price. The term "color" means "color capability" and does not imply that a monitor or TV set is included.)
Computer	

(Very Low Priced)

COMMODORE VIC20	5K RAM, cartridge player, color
RADIO SHACK MC–10	4K RAM, color

(Low Priced)

ATARI 600XL and 800XL	16K RAM, (64K for 800XL), cartridge player, color
COMMODORE 64	64K RAM, cartridge player, color, music synthesizer
RADIO SHACK COLOR COMPUTER 2	16K RAM, cartridge player, color
SINCLAIR QL*	128K RAM, color, two high-speed tape storage drives, word processing and other software (including graphics, spreadsheet, and database management), cartridge player

* Not available in stores. Mail-order only. Sinclair Research, Ltd., Boston.

B. MEDIUM-PRICED	
Computer	**Basic System**

ACORN	64K RAM, color, built-in word-processing software in ROM, music synthesizer
ATARI 1450XLD	64K RAM, cartridge player, color, voice synthesizer, one disk drive
COLECO ADAM	80K RAM, cartridge player, color, high-speed tape storage drive, letter-quality printer, joysticks, built-in word-processing software in ROM
IBM PCjr (entry model)	64K RAM, cartridge player, color
SANYO MBC-550	128K RAM, color, one disk drive, word-processing and other software

FIGURE B–1 / **Basic Configuration** (continued)

C. HIGH-PRICED SYSTEMS	
Computer	**Basic System**
APPLE IIe*	64K RAM, color
APPLE MACINTOSH	128K RAM, one disk drive, monitor, mouse, voice synthesizer, music synthesizer
FRANKLIN ACE 1000*	64K RAM, color
KAYPRO II	64K RAM, two disk drives, monitor, word-processing and other software
IBM PCjr (expanded model)	128K RAM, cartridge player, color, one disk drive
IBM PC	64K RAM, one disk drive
MINDSET	64K RAM, color, advanced graphics software and hardware, cartridge player

* NOTE: The Apple IIe and the Franklin were reduced in price as we went to press. They now fall within the medium-priced category. At the same time, Apple introduced a portable computer called the Apple IIc. It resembles the Apple IIe, but contains a built-in disk drive. An optional "flat screen" and/or a mouse can be added. Unlike the Apple IIe, this computer does not have "expansion slots" for additional boards that let you add such features as CP/M or a music synthesizer. The Apple IIc fits into the high-priced category.

FIGURE B–2 / **Screen**

A. LOW-PRICED COMPUTERS			
Computer	**Columns and Rows**	**Can Attach Monitor?**	**Comments**
(Very Low Priced)			
COMMODORE VIC20	22x23	Yes	Large letters can be helpful for young children Very limited for word processing
RADIO SHACK MC–10	32x16	No	
(Low Priced)			
ATARI 600XL & 800XL	40x24	Yes	Excellent for games Exceptionally sharp picture signal Does not interfere with nearby radio & TV reception Suitable for simple word processing
COMMODORE 64	40x25	Yes	Versatile Portable version available (Executive 64)
RADIO SHACK COLOR COMPUTER 2	32x16	No	Picture often appears harsh or ragged; quality varies with TV set used, especially in colors obtained
SINCLAIR QL	80x25 (40 to 60 columns with TV)	Yes	Easy-to-use word processor included System originally intended for business users Monitor needed; TV interface being developed Uses windows and icons (see footnote for Macintosh)

FIGURE B–2 / **Screen** (continued)

B. MEDIUM-PRICED COMPUTERS			
Computer	**Columns and Rows**	**Can Attach Monitor?**	**Comments**
ACORN	80x25	Yes	Screen acceptable for all levels of word processing
ATARI 1450XLD	40x24	Yes	Exceptionally sharp picture signal System is suitable for simple to intermediate-level word processing
COLECO ADAM	36x24	Yes	Screen acceptable for simple word processing 80-column option to be available in future Company currently advises against using monitor hookup Sharper picture reportedly obtainable by using much shorter cord to connect keyboard with CPU
IBM PCjr (entry model)	40x25	Yes	Screen capability can be upgraded to 80 columns Extra charge for ability to attach monitor System is limited to very simple word processing unless upgraded with disk
SANYO MBC–550	80x25	Yes	Suitable for advanced word processing Monitor needed; cannot attach TV Runs many IBM-compatible word-processing programs

FIGURE B–2 / **Screen** (continued)

	C. HIGH-PRICED COMPUTERS		
Computer	**Columns and Rows**	**Can Attach Monitor?**	**Comments**
APPLE IIe	40x24	Yes	With optional 80 columns, suitable for advanced word processing
APPLE MACINTOSH	80x24	No	9-inch monitor is built in Very clear image because of high-resolution ability Very flexible display (type fonts and style range from 8 pt. to 72 pt. type) Uses screen windows* and icons**
FRANKLIN ACE 1000	40x24	Yes	Optional 80-column board
KAYPRO II	80x24	No	9-inch green monitor is built in Portable computer
IBM PCjr (expanded model)	80x25	Yes	Screen good for word processing, but system is limited by keyboard and one-disk maximum (unless third-party accessories are purchased)

* Windows are screen divisions that are helpful when working on several tasks at once.

** Icons are pictorial symbols for computer operations such as store, retrieve, print.

FIGURE B–2 / **Screen** (continued)

| C. **HIGH-PRICED COMPUTERS** (continued) | | | |
Computer	Columns and Rows	Can Attach Monitor?	Comments
IBM PC	80x25	Yes	Color text mode is hard to read; black-and-white text mode is exceptionally clear Cannot attach TV Suitable for advanced word processing
MINDSET	80x25	Yes	Very clear image because of high-resolution ability Can attach color or black-and-white TV RGB monitor needed for higher-resolution modes Runs many IBM-compatible word-processing programs

FIGURE B–3 / **Color and Graphics**

A. LOW-PRICED COMPUTERS			
Computer	**Number of Colors**	**Highest Resolution**	**Comments**
(Very Low Priced)			
COMMODORE VIC20	16	176x184	Elaborate character-set graphics
RADIO SHACK MC–10	8	64x32	16 character-set graphics keys
(Low Priced)			
ATARI 600XL & 800XL	256	320x192	See Atari 1450XLD
COMMODORE 64	16	320x200	Elaborate character-set graphics 16 colors at 320x200, but only 4 colors in each 8x8 region 8 sprites
RADIO SHACK COLOR COM-PUTER 2	9	256x192	2 colors at 256x192; 4 colors at 128x192; 8 colors at 64x32 Easy-to-use BASIC commands for drawing lines and circles and for filling areas with color Square character-set graphics
SINCLAIR QL	8	512x256 with monitor	256x256 with TV Each character can be a different color with monitor 16 character-set graphics keys 4 colors at 512x256 (black, white, green, red); 8 colors at 256x256

FIGURE B–3 / **Color and Graphics** (continued)

B. MEDIUM-PRICED COMPUTERS			
Computer	**Number of Colors**	**Highest Resolution***	**Comments**
ACORN	16	640x200	Good graphics capabilities 2 colors at 640x200; 4 colors at 320x200; 16 colors at 160x200 Can overlay shapes
ATARI 1450XLD	256	320x192	Versatile graphics 2 colors at 320x192; 4 colors at 160x192; 8 colors at 160x96 Good character-set graphics 256 possible shades (16 basic colors times 16 intensities) Optional graphics tablet
COLECO ADAM	16	255x191	Good for animation 32 sprites
IBM PCjr (entry model)	16	640x200	Good graphics capabilities 4 colors at 640x200; 16 colors at 320x200
SANYO MBC–550	8	640x200	8 colors at 640x200 Color-graphics software included

* Resolutions higher than 320x200 require a monitor.

FIGURE B–3 / **Color and Graphics** (continued)

C. HIGH-PRICED COMPUTERS

Computer	Number of Colors	Highest Resolution*	Comments
APPLE IIe	16	280x192 (b&w)	6 colors at 140x192
APPLE MACINTOSH	none	512x342 (b&w)	Very advanced (and fast) graphics capabilities and graphics software (black-and-white only)
FRANKLIN ACE 1000	16	280x192 (b&w)	6 colors at 140x192
KAYPRO II	160x100 (b&w)	none	Text oriented; not suitable for games Limited b&w graphics
IBM PCjr (expanded model)	16	640x200	4 colors at 640x200; 16 colors at 320x200
IBM PC	16	640x200 (b&w)	Color-capacity option 4 colors at 320x200
MINDSET	512	640x400	2 colors at 640x400; 16 colors at 320x200 Extremely fast graphics Excellent for animation Can "mix colors" on screen to create new ones Needs expansion memory, additional software package, and mouse or tablet to make drawings easily 3 graphics packages available: Designer, Lumena, and Four Point Graphics Plus

* Resolutions higher than 320x200 require a monitor.

FIGURE B–4 / **Keyboard***

<table>
<tr><td colspan="4">A. LOW-PRICED COMPUTERS</td></tr>
<tr><th>Computer</th><th>Type of
Keys</th><th>User-
Definable
Function
Keys</th><th>Comments</th></tr>
<tr><td colspan="4">(Very Low Priced)</td></tr>
<tr><td>COMMODORE
VIC20</td><td>Full-size
keys</td><td>8</td><td>4 function keys used
with and without shift</td></tr>
<tr><td>RADIO SHACK
MC—10</td><td>Small-size
keys</td><td>0</td><td>Small keyboard

Special keys for BASIC
commands

Not suitable for touch
typing</td></tr>
<tr><td colspan="4">(Low Priced)</td></tr>
<tr><td>ATARI 600XL &
800XL</td><td>Full-size
keys</td><td>4</td><td></td></tr>
<tr><td>COMMODORE
64</td><td>Full-size
keys</td><td>8</td><td>4 function keys used
with and without shift</td></tr>
<tr><td>RADIO SHACK
COLOR COM-
PUTER 2</td><td>Full-size
keys</td><td>0</td><td></td></tr>
<tr><td>SINCLAIR QL</td><td>Full-size
keys</td><td>5</td><td></td></tr>
</table>

* All computers in each price range have a typewriter keyboard layout.

FIGURE B–4 / **Keyboard** (continued)

B. MEDIUM-PRICED COMPUTERS

Computer	Type of Keys	User-Definable Function Keys	Comments
ACORN	Full-size keys	40	10 function keys used with and without shift and control keys
ATARI 1450XLD	Full-size keys	4	
COLECO ADAM	Full-size keys	6	
IBM PCjr (entry model)	Small-size keys	0**	Cordless keyboard Long narrow keys Not good for touch typing
SANYO MBC–550	Full-size keys	15	5 function keys used with and without shift and control keys Detachable keyboard with cord Separate numeric keypad

** See footnote to Figure 3–7.

FIGURE B–4 / **Keyboard** (continued)

	C. HIGH-PRICED COMPUTERS		
Computer	**Type of Keys**	**User-Definable Function Keys**	**Comments**
APPLE IIe	Full-size keys	0	2 all-purpose keys similar to function keys
APPLE MACINTOSH	Full-size keys	0	Mouse (control device) replaces many keyboard functions for ease of use
FRANKLIN ACE 1000	Full-size keys	0	Separate numeric keypad
KAYPRO II	Full-size keys	0	Detachable keyboard Separate numeric keypad
IBM PCjr (expanded model)	Small-size keys	0*	Cordless keyboard Long narrow keys Not good for touch typing
IBM PC	Full-size keys	10	Detachable keyboard, with cord Separate numeric keypad Poor keyboard layout, especially for children
MINDSET	Full-size keys	10	Detachable keyboard, with cord

* See footnote to Figure 3–7.

FIGURE B–5 / **Sound**

A. LOW-PRICED COMPUTERS			
Computer	**Number of Voices**	**Number of Octaves**	**Comments**
(Very Low Priced)			
COMMODORE VIC20	4	3	3 voices for music; 1 voice for sound effects Not controlled through simple BASIC commands
RADIO SHACK MC—10	1	3	
(Low Priced)			
ATARI 600XL & 800XL	4	3	Easy to use through BASIC
COMMODORE 64	3	9	Sophisticated but not easy to use Music synthesizer with ADSR control included Programmable filters Hi-fi capabilities No easy control through BASIC commands except with special software*
RADIO SHACK COLOR COMPUTER 2	1	3	Easy to use
SINCLAIR QL	None	None	No sound except beep tone Multichannel sound accessory will be offered later

* A special cartridge called "Simon's Basic" simplifies the use of sound and graphics.

FIGURE B–5 / **Sound** (continued)

B. MEDIUM-PRICED COMPUTERS			
Computer	Number of Voices	Number of Octaves	Comments
ACORN	4	5	Sophisticated and easy to use Music synthesizer included Elaborate ADSR control Auto repeat Control from BASIC commands
ATARI 1450XLD	4	3	Music easy to use Voice synthesizer included
COLECO ADAM	3	5	
IBM PCjr (entry model)	3	7	Optional voice synthesizer
SANYO MBC–550	None	None	No sound except beep tones

FIGURE B–5 / **Sound** (continued)

C. HIGH-PRICED COMPUTERS			
Computers	**Number of Voices**	**Number of Octaves**	**Comments**
APPLE IIe	1	9	Optional piano-like keyboard and music synthesizer available from third party Third party voice synthesizer available
APPLE MACINTOSH	4	8	Voice synthesizer included Music synthesizer with ADSR included
FRANKLIN ACE 1000	1	9	Third party voice synthesizer available
KAYPRO II	None	None	No sound except beep tone
IBM PCjr (expanded model)	3	7	Optional voice synthesizer
IBM PC	None	None	No sound except beep tone Optional voice synthesizer Built-in speaker can be used by accessories to produce sound
MINDSET	6	8	3 modes of use: 3, 4, and 6 voices; fewer voices gives better sound quality Stereo output accessory will be available

FIGURE B–6 / **Storage**

A. LOW-PRICED COMPUTERS			
Computers	**Accepts Cartridges?**	**Capacity Per Disk**	**Comments**
(Very Low Priced)			
COMMODORE VIC20	Yes	170K	
RADIO SHACK MC–10	No	No disk	
(Low Priced)			
ATARI 600XL & 800Xl	Yes	127K	Can have total of 4 disk drives
COMMODORE 64	Yes	170K	
RADIO SHACK COLOR COMPUTER 2	Yes	156K	Can have total of 4 disk drives
SINCLAIR QL	Yes	No disk	Includes 2 high-speed storage tapes (100K each) called Microdrives Can have a total of 8 Microdrives Interface to third-party disk drives being developed Will not accept Timex Sinclair cartridges from previous models

FIGURE B–6 / **Storage** (continued)

	B. MEDIUM-PRICED COMPUTERS		
Computer	**Accepts Cartridges?**	**Capacity Per Disk**	**Comments**
ACORN	No	400K	Can store long documents for word processing
ATARI 1450XLD	Yes	254K	Includes one built-in disk drive Can add more disk drives
COLECO ADAM	Yes	No disk	Uses high-speed storage tape (256K) One tape drive included Disk announced for future
IBM PCjr (entry model)	Yes	360K	Upgradable to one disk drive
SANYO MBC–550	No	160K	Later model (MBC–550-2) offers 320K One disk drive included

FIGURE B–6 / **Storage** (continued)

C. HIGH-PRICED COMPUTERS			
Computer	**Accepts Cartridges?**	**Capacity Per Disk**	**Comments**
APPLE IIe	No	143K	
APPLE MACINTOSH	No	400K	One 3½-inch drive included
FRANKLIN ACE 1000	No	143K	
KAYPRO II	No	200K	Two disk drives included; built into case for portability KayPro 4 version has 400K per disk
IBM PCjr (expanded model)	Yes	360K	One disk drive included Cannot add a second drive; this limits the level of sophistication of word processing and other tools to an intermediate level
IBM PC	No	180K and 360K	180K if you use a "single-sided" floppy disk; 360K if you use "double-sided"
MINDSET	Yes	360K	Can have 2 disk drives

FIGURE B–7 / **CPU and Memory**

A. LOW-PRICED COMPUTERS				
Computer	CPU Chip	Standard RAM Memory	Maximum RAM Memory	Comments
(Very Low Priced)				
COMMO-DORE VIC20	6502 (8-bit)	5K	32K	
RADIO SHACK MC–10	6803 (8-bit)	4K	20K	
(Low Priced)				
ATARI 600XL & 800XL	6502 (8-bit)	16K or 64K	64K	600XL is 16K minimum; 800 XL is 64K
COMMO-DORE 64	6510 (8-bit)	64K	64K	Optional Z–80 CPU for CP/M
RADIO SHACK COLOR COM-PUTER 2	6809 (8-bit)	16K	64K	
SINCLAIR QL	68008 (32-bit)	128K	640K	QDOS operating system Fast processor Sufficient memory to run large financial spread sheet programs Good potential for statistical and scientific calculations Operating system can run several tasks at once, and can divide screen into viewing windows

FIGURE B–7 / **CPU and Memory** (continued)

B. MEDIUM-PRICED COMPUTERS				
Computer	CPU Chip	Standard RAM Memory	Maximum RAM Memory	Comments
ACORN	6502 (8-bit)	64K	256K with added 16-bit processor	Can add other processors: • second 6502 • Z–80B • 16032 (16-bit)
ATARI 1450XLD	6502 (8-bit)	64K	64K	
COLECO ADAM	Z–80A (8-bit)	80K	144K	With 80K RAM, actual work space available to user is 32K for word processing and 40K for BASIC programming In future, will run CP/M
IBM PCjr (entry model)	8088 (16-bit)	64K	128K	Runs MS-DOS (PC-DOS version 2.1)
SANYO MBC–550	8088 (16-bit)	128K	256K	Runs MS-DOS (All comments on IBM PC in this chart apply here) Runs faster than the IBM PC because of design differences

FIGURE B–7 / **CPU and Memory** (continued)

C. HIGH-PRICED COMPUTERS				
Computer	CPU Chip	Standard RAM Memory	Maximum RAM Memory	Comments
APPLE IIe	6502 (8-bit)	64K	128K	Expandable to 512K with third-party board Optional Z–80 for CP/M from third-party manufacturers
APPLE MACINTOSH	68000 (32-bit)	128K	128K (512K later)	May have UNIX available later Has multi-task-ing, windows, and icons
FRANKLIN ACE 1000	6502 (8-bit)	64K	64K	Expandable to 512K with third-party board Optional Z–80 card for CP/M
KAYPRO II	Z–80A	64K	64K	Runs CP/M
IBM PCjr (expanded model)	8088 (16-bit)	128K	128K	Runs MS-DOS (PC-DOS version 2.1)
IBM PC	8088 (16-bit)	64K	640K	Large memory and 16-bit power make it suitable for integrated packages like Lotus 1, 2, 3 and for statistical work and word processing of long documents Has 8087 co-processor option for very fast calculations if desired Runs MS-DOS (PC-DOS versions 2.0 and 2.1) Can run CP/M–86

FIGURE B–7 / **CPU and Memory** (continued)

C. HIGH-PRICED COMPUTERS (continued)				
Computer	CPU Chip	Standard RAM Memory	Maximum RAM Memory	Comments
MINDSET	80186 (16-bit)	64K (includes 32K frame buffer)	256K	Runs MS-DOS Very fast processor Very fast graphics produced by two graphics co-processors and by use of 32K RAM "screen buffer" that holds images

Index